An Investor's Guide to Portfolio Strategy Development

THEORY, TECHNIQUES, & KNOW-HOW FOR FINANCIAL ADVISORS AND INVESTORS

Brandon H. VanLandingham

Book Layout ©2015 BookDesignTemplates.com

Book Cover Design: Ben DuBois

Edited by: Charlotte Estep

An Investor's Guide to Portfolio Strategy Development/
Brandon H. VanLandingham. —1st ed.

ISBN-13: 978-1507871881
ISBN-10: 1507871880

Contents

To my wife Patricia, for always providing encouragement.

The market is not a weighing machine, on which the value of each issue is recorded by an exact and impersonal mechanism, in accordance with its specific qualities. Rather should we say the market is a voting machine, whereon countless individuals register choices which are the product partly of reason and partly of emotion.

—Ben Graham

Introduction

There is no reason why an individual cannot make money investing in stocks or other markets. However, there are many reasons why most people do not. Investing is like anything else we attempt; we must put in the time and do necessary homework in order to gain knowledge. The knowledge we obtain is transferred directly to action. Let me give you an analogy that I hope will help make sense of how this book is written and what I hope readers are able to take away.

Think of investing in terms playing Black Jack. When walking into a casino, possible gamblers know without having to be told that the odds are stacked in the house's favor. For most investors, the market as a whole has the advantage. However, suppose an individual has spent several months or even years honing card counting skills. Now the odds are stacked in the gambler's favor at least that is what he or she is hoping. Being able to count cards is similar to knowing when to buy a stock and when to sell a stock as well as knowing when to cut losses. Technical analysis is equivalent to card counting. Just as in counting cards, technical analysis does not guarantee success; it helps to increase the odds of success. Counting cards informs when to increase bets and when to leave the table. Technical analysis helps determine when to buy and when to sell a security. The skill level of the card counter will determine his or her overall success and the same goes for the technical analyst. Anyone can learn to count cards just as anyone can learn technical analysis.

What separates this book from other investment books, especially books on technical analysis? First, what is more important than counting cards when entering a casino ready to play Black Jack? It is knowing which tables are hot and which tables are not. Knowing which tables are hot is difficult and is equivalent to knowing which stocks are worth an investment. The skills used to know which table to sit at are equivalent to valuation skills. Valuation techniques help an investor identify a good investment and add another dimension to the probability of success. Gamblers can count cards all night long, but if the table is cold, they can still lose everything. Remember that a good company does not necessarily make a good investment. Investors can buy a great company's stock, but if the price is too high they could still lose money.

This book has been written, not only for the individual investor attempting to gain knowledge, but also to expand the knowledge of even the most astute advisors with whom most individuals trust to manage their life savings. It is intended for all investors interested in investing and covers several topics from fundamental analysis to technical analysis. Very few books have encompassed the different investment philosophies of valuation and technical analysis as well as portfolio construction and management. The governing principle of this book is to guide investors through the minutia of investment philosophy and theories in order for them to develop their own investment philosophy. There are hundreds if not thousands of books stating they can teach how to "beat the market" or simplify investing, but the truth is they typically tell only one side of the story. My goal is to provide as much background information as I can in order to help manage assets in the best possible way FOR EACH INVESTOR. I hope to at least shed light on the arguments for and against active and passive management so that advisors can better communicate with their clients and clients can ask the right questions in order to seek out the right financial counsel regarding the management of their financial assets.

This book is written in four parts. The first part will identify the type of investor each person is or should be. An active investor believes individual investors are capable of outperforming a benchmark such as the S&P 500. Another investor believes that consistently outperforming at a benchmark is a zero sum game and that attempting to do so is a waste of time. Part one of this book should provide positive ideas as to how money should be managed based on expectations of returns. I will review the Efficient Market Hypothesis (EMH) as well as Behavioral Finance as it pertains to human rationality and irrationality. I will define several investor biases that all investors suffer from. Part two addresses different valuation models used by investors to determine intrinsic value. These include the Dividend Discount model, Free Cash Flow models, and Residual Income models. Examining the pros and cons of using such models as well as how each are calculated will demystify the processes. The third part involves portfolio management techniques for both active and passive investing strategies. As this text will explain, there is no explicitly right or wrong way to manage a portfolio. It is more about expectations of risk and returns that determines ultimate success or failure. Part four takes an in-depth look at technical analysis which can be one of the most viable tools in any investor's tool kit. During the financial crisis of 2008 there was little that could be done in avoiding the collapse. Almost every equity style box, from large cap value to small cap growth was down more than 30%. However, had an investor understood technical analysis and developed a rules based approach to investing, much of the crisis could have been avoided through the process of keeping emotions in check and investing in a more rational way.

This book is not for the professional investor alone and has been intentionally written in such a way that the astute individual with a willingness to learn can find this book extremely useful. The individual investor has now been thrust in the driver's seat of his or her retirement. Think back 40 years ago; most companies offered defined benefit plans for their employees. Now 401ks and IRAs are the mainstream for individual investors. I strongly suggest that most individuals seek out professional guidance considering most do not have the time or skill level to properly manage a portfolio. This book can be used as a guide for the individual to have an independent mind when considering different professional advisors to employ. If reading this book has helped an investor decide on how assets should be managed, that investor will be informed about how to locate investment advisors who are capable of implementing an individualized investment plan.

The goal of this book is to help individual investors or an advisor managing the assets on behalf of investors to design and implement a solid investment strategy. An investor must hear both sides of an argument in order to make sound investment decisions. I hope this book serves as a reference and a guide to implement the investment strategy or strategies that are best for the investor and the advisor.

[PART I]

Are Markets Efficient?

W hat type of investor is the average individual? Sounds like a simple question, right? I would assume that most individuals that have taken the time to read this book believe in the potential of active investing and hope to gain the knowledge to become successful. Debate has raged for decades as to which style of investing is best, active or passive. Based on current evidence for both passive and active investing, it actually comes down to a personal decision. I cannot say that by following any of the advice in this book will guarantee an investor will beat the market over an investing career. There are too many variables. Emotions will likely play the biggest role in investment outcomes over any other variable. What I will present are the arguments to both sides and let the individual decide whether to invest resources using an active strategy or a passive one. This topic is so neutral that the 2013 Nobel Prize was awarded to two economist that are polar opposites. Robert Shiller the author of <u>Irrational Exuberance</u> believes markets are inefficient because humans are inefficient and often irrational and that active management can outperform markets over time. Eugene Fama, who coined the phrase Efficient Markets in the 1960's was the other winner, and believes markets are efficient and anyone who beats the market over any period does so by luck. The Nobel Prize is based on a lifetime of work and overall contribution to the understanding of economics. This makes the case for either side more difficult as both sides have arguments that stand up to the most rigid tests.

Individuals who have been students of financial markets for any period of time have heard the Efficient Market Hypothesis. Whether an investor's belief is based on that hypothesis or not will determine how to structure an investment strategy. The early works of Eugene Fama and the other pioneers of the Efficient Market Theory are rather convincing. Closely watching a stock at the moment it reports earnings that are either a surprise to the upside or downside reveals that the news regarding a stock is priced-in extremely fast as though markets are efficient. However, watching that stock closely for the next several minutes to hours may reveal that after a drastic rise or fall when the news initially hits the price move may reverse course throughout the rest of the trading day. In that moment the markets were perhaps a little irrational. It is almost as if the markets are efficient on action but inefficient when it comes to the impact regarding new information. I will provide information for both arguments in hopes that investors are able to make an educated decision about whether markets are efficient and cannot yield profit or whether it is possible to create an active investment strategy that can overtime outperform a passive strategy.

[1]

Efficient Market Hypothesis

In order to make an informed decision on the appropriate investment approach whether it is passive or active, it is critical to fully understand the arguments for each side. Let us first take a look at the Efficient Market Hypothesis (EMH). Larry Blum and Steven Drulauf (2007), give one of the best broad comparisons between EMH and behavioral economists.

The efficient markets hypothesis (EMH) maintains that market prices fully reflect all available information. Developed independently by Paul A. Samuelson and Eugene F. Fama in the 1960's, this idea has been applied extensively to theoretical models and empirical studies of financial securities prices, generating considerable controversy as well as fundamental insights into the price-discovery process. The most enduring critique comes from psychologist and behavioral economists who argue that the EMH is based on counterfactual assumptions regarding human behavior, that is, rationality. Recent advances in evolutionary psychology and the cognitive neurosciences

may be able to reconcile the EMH with behavioral anomalies.

The foundations that EMH are built upon are information and
extreme competition. Material information introduced to the
market will likely change an investment's price either for the
good or the bad. For example, suppose Caterpillar Inc. receives
an order from China for one million new D10 Dozers. If we
receive this information legally and before anyone else is able
to act on it, we will be able to make a nice profit. Investors are
extremely competitive towards this type of information which
is considered material. (For simplicity we will define "Material
Information" as information that will cause the stock price to
either rise or fall.) EMH implies that all information that is
available is already priced into a stock. So the dozer order from
China would be priced-in immediately, and by the time the information is circulated, the price move will have already happened. This may sound extreme and in reality it is a little
extreme that is why there are three broad schools of thought
on EMH.

They are:

> **Weak form EMH:** *All past information is reflected in*
> *market/stock prices*
>
> **Semi-strong form EMH:** *All publically available infor-*
> *mation has been priced into stocks.*
>
> **Strong form EMH:** *Current market prices incorporate*
> *ALL public and private information.*

If EMH is true, price changes are unpredictable on any time-
table and there is no way to profit from new information. An
example of this is in takeovers or buyouts. Look at a chart of
the company that is being bought, and if the price is a premium
to their current price, there will likely be a gap in the stock
price. This means that the current owners of the stock will not

sell the stock for less than the new premium and this new information was instantly priced in. Think of it from the perspective of the current owners of the stock. When new information informs the public that the market price is undervalued, holders would have to be stupid to sell their stock for less than this new information says the company is worth. That is why there can be a price gap on a stock chart. If this is in fact the case, the best investment strategy is to be passive in which investors would buy the entire stock market through some type of low cost indexing funds. This ensures the market's best return; however, the downside is the investor will also receive all the worst returns as well. If one cannot beat the market, the best hope is to match it is the mantra for EMH enthusiast. Advocates for EMH believe that the out-performance by professional money managers in any given year is pure luck. One analogy used by EMH advocates is to put 100 people in a room each with a quarter. These "investors" are to flip the coin 100 times. EMH advocates point toward basic statistics that say there will be a small minority that will flip a "heads" over 75% of the time. Does this make them professional coin flippers or simply lucky. This minority was in fact lucky, and skill was not involved.

Information on Wall Street has been said to be more valuable than gold. Having information that no one else has is invaluable as an investor and at times is illegal. This intense competition for information is exactly what put Raj Rajaratnam in prison for insider trading. If markets were efficient, people would stop searching for information that can give them an edge. Grossman and Stiglitz (1980) state that if markets are completely efficient and there is no possible way to exploit new information, there is no possible way to profit from additional information. If this were true, there would be no reason to trade markets and the markets will eventually fail. The belief behind the theory is that such inefficiencies in the markets must exist to compensate traders/investors for the cost to trade and research information.

Does this reality provoke thought? We all wish it was easy to make a decision and hope for proof so that we know with certainty how we should invest our resources. As with any theory, there is room for judgment just as it is difficult to disprove EMH. Since there is no certainty, investors are typically influenced by "professionals." Professional money managers would have investors believe that they have the ability to make more money than an individual can make investing passively. This may or may not be true. One thing is certain: an active management strategy will from time to time, no matter how good, underperform its benchmarks.

Campbell and Shiller (1988) and Fama and French (1989) both showed varying degrees of market anomalies that on the surface look as though they have the ability to predict broad stock market returns. Fama and French show how the spread between high grade bonds and low grade bonds can be used to predict stock market returns. Campbell and Shiller show that the earnings yield of the broad market has the ability to forecast stock market returns as well. Kane, Bodie, and Marcus (2009) state that this does not show evidence of market inefficiency, rather it shows that these varying fundamental factors can predict the risk premium for stocks. This makes sense. When stock prices are depressed, the dividend yield and the earnings yield will be higher. This will translate into a higher risk premium, which is the difference between the expected market returns and the risk free rate of return. A higher risk premium shows that expected market returns are high and will likely result in higher stock market returns over time. If a stock is trading at $20 and it paid a $2 dividend, it has a 10% dividend yield. If the stock price falls to $10 and the company maintains the $2 dividend, the company now has a dividend yield of 20%. We can use the same analogy for the broad markets, such as the S&P 500. When the dividend yield rises or is high compared to the risk free rate, we can expect that the market is on sale and it is a good time to invest. The thing is the market can remain on sale for extended periods of time. What we typically see is the market based on current assumptions tends to appear fairly valued, not cheap and not expensive. Even when the market appears expensive, we can see it stay this way for long periods of time. Currently (2015) the market appears expensive when using Robert Shiller's Cyclically Adjusted Price to Earnings (CAPE). It has been signaling that the market is expecting low returns since 2012. However, in 2013 the market returned over 30%. Most investment gurus appearing in the media were screaming that the market was now overvalued and expected a correction in the first part of 2014. Did that happen? No. The S&P returned over 13% in 2014. So market returns may be predictable over say ten year periods in context to some point in time, but the market still appears mostly efficient. Even if we can predict that market returns will be lower or higher from current levels over an extended period of time, we still cannot predict if markets will be positive or negative over the next day, week, month, or year. In this context, markets are still for the most part efficient.

The last argument I will make for efficient markets involves capital markets and how monetary assets are allocated. Capital markets in theory are supposed to provide capital where capital is most needed. If the value to build a new plant exceeds the cost of building the plant, money will flow to this project due to the value it produces for the providers of capital. If markets were inefficient we would expect that the use of capital would also be inefficient. Kane, Bodie, and Marcus (2013) explain that if stock prices are consistently overpriced and underpriced, overpriced companies will be able to obtain additional capital at a lower cost than other companies, and the undervalued companies will possibly have to forego expansion and investment opportunities that could add significant value because the cost of raising additional capital was too high. The flip side of this is that we have seen in history a misallocation of resources such as the technology bubble in the late 1990s and the housing bubble in the late 2000s. What does this say about resource allocation? Does this show market inefficiency? Not necessarily. Remember that the market reflects all available information, not all available perfect information. Think about the period leading up to the housing crisis as a period where all available information was not accurate or complete, but once new information regarding the situation occurred, the market responded quickly.

We need to keep in mind what the EMH is actually about. It is not about perfect information. If the market is responding to information that is inaccurate, it is still an efficient market. This is why I believe markets are "mostly" efficient. As an active money manager, I believe it is possible that the market can be informationally efficient, but this information may not be completely accurate. This is the key to active management: investors must form an opinion based on public information that differs from the consensus and on average be correct. The markets are pricing in information that an analyst needs to believe is not compete or does not tell the entire story.

A relatively new theory put forth by Andrew Lo (2004) is titled The Adaptive Market Hypothesis (AMH), which is an adaptation to EMH. Mr. Lo states that AMH:

> ...is based on an evolutionary approach to economic iterations, as well as some recent research in the cognitive neurosciences that has been transforming and revitalizing the intersection of psychology and economics.

Lo's theory is grounded in the works of biology and evolution. He implies that even our own human behavior is not intrinsic and exogenous, but actually evolves by natural selection. Natural selection as we have all learned in biology is the gradual process by which biological traits become either more or less common in a population as a function of the effect of inherited traits on the differential reproductive success of organisms. This makes sense for nearly all aspects of our lives and not only biology. For example when my nephew is old enough to learn about money and investing, and if I am privileged enough to teach him, he will learn everything that I know about the markets. I hope that he is able to take these methods and principles and improve upon them just as I have done. The things of the past have either improved or disappeared. Think for example about how trades and technical analysis are processed. It has been only twenty years since the first trades were placed electronically on the New York Stock Exchange, and now nearly all exchanges around the world process trades in this manner. If persons born in the past thirty years study technical analysis, they will be amazed to realize that all charts used to be created with graph paper. But today with a click of the mouse anyone can look at any style chart, whether it is point and figure or candlestick, in seconds without sharpening a pencil. So because Mr. Lo's theory has yet to garner much in the way of academic approval, although it is gaining ground, it is easy to see how this evolutionary approach is a viable alternative theory to EMH.

He goes on to say:

> If, on the other hand, the environment changes, it should come as no surprise that the heuristics of the old environment are not necessarily well suited to the new. In such cases, we observe "behavioral biases"—actions that are apparently ill advised in the context in which we observe them. But rather than label-

ing such behavior irrational, we should recognize that suboptimal behavior is not unlikely when we take heuristics out of their evolutionary context. A more accurate term for such behavior might be "maladaptive." The flopping of a fish on dry land may seem strange and unproductive, but underwater, the same motions are capable of propelling the fish away from its predators.

It is interesting to see how efficient markets and behavioral finance are able to intertwine in such a way to explain and try to make logical sense of what seems so illogical. The AMH theory attempts to explain why we see behavioral biases in financial decisions and markets not as irrational behavior but as rational behavior affected by the current state of the environment investors are currently experiencing as well as adaptive so that only the fittest survive. Lo states that emotions are part of the reward and punishment system that filters down to the most advantageous behaviors surviving and improves learning efficiency. He concludes that since the financial markets are so competitive and the rewards for the behaviors most sharpened in the current environment are financially enhanced the most, the most logical explanation is a so called "survival of the richest," Darwinian selection process that hones the profile of the successful trader. Unsuccessful traders are eventually weeded out and eliminated from the investing population after suffering a certain level of losses.

After several decades of research and published papers as well as some heated debates, economists are still unable to reach a consensus as to whether markets are, in fact, efficient. Reading through the rest of this book and internalizing its messages, will I hope determine the best way to manage resources. The next chapter will reveal the way to make a "rational" decision as to whether markets are efficient. This will be the most important financial decision any investor will make, above what stock to pick or when to buy and sell. Deciding on BELIEFS about financial markets will determine overall success and expectations in investing endeavors.

[2]

Behavioral Finance

In the previous chapter I discussed arguments both for and against EMH. There have been many articles written on EMH, so I did not feel it was necessary to elaborate intensively on the subject. However I feel that Behavioral Finance is something some may have heard of, but I feel it is not nearly as well publicized. For those reasons I have chosen to dedicate an entire chapter on the subject, and it may be that I reveal that I am quite partial to the subject as well. If there is underlying evidence that humans often are unable to make rational decisions when money is involved, there may be underlying evidence that EMH does not necessarily hold true all of the time. I will explain several behavioral biases that investors face and by doing this show that even if markets exhibit signs of efficiency, they are also prone to inefficiency caused by behavioral biases that all humans have developed over millions of years to help make decisions to preserve life. If we are able to see behavioral biases in decision making processes, we at least have an argument that markets may not be efficient, and it is possible to take advantage of market inefficiencies to increase returns.

When I was a young boy growing up in Woodward, Oklahoma, I remember my parents constantly telling me not to do something because I would get hurt, but for some reason I would have to experience the pain on my own even when it was demonstrated what would happen. I remember one particular event when I was about nine or ten years old when my best friend and I were running wild on his grandparents' farm. There was an electric fence that kept the cows and other livestock from escaping that was nearly always turned off. I guess the cows learn faster than a ten-year-old boy. My friend approached the wire cautiously like he had done thousands of times and slowly reached out his finger as if by being slow made a difference whether the fence was on or off. When his finger made contact with the fence, I was certain that he was having a seizure. Even after the electricity let him go, he was shaking and screaming and running around in pain. Now, some would think that after seeing this display of utter pain, I would learn not to touch the fence. Well, not this brilliant ten-year-old. In about the same fashion as my friend, I walked up and had to see for myself. Moron... would be a word most people would use to describe my behavior. However, let me share a secret; most of us act in the same fashion but maybe not in such grand fashion as my example.

I want to discuss this particular behavior first in part so that once this chapter is read and internalized we remember that we all suffer from behavioral biases that inhibit investing ability, and knowing that these biases exist can help to minimize their power. This first behavior has been described in detail in the paper, "The tree of experience in the forest of information: Overweighing experience relative to observed information" by Uri Simonsohn, Niklas Karlsson, George Loewenstein, and Dan Ariely (2008). Their research concluded that we weigh information we attain from experience more than we weigh information we only observe. This is extremely useful in its application for investors. Benjamin Franklin once opined, "Experience is a dear teacher, but fools will learn at no other." In my opinion, in order to succeed in investing we must learn to follow statistics as opposed to emotional information. By doing this we will increase the probability of success. I want to address this bias first because the other biases that follow should not be taken with a grain of salt, they should be studied diligently. I have worked with other advisors and no matter how many times I explained the biases that we all face, they seem to have to experience a phenomenon first-hand in order to realize the magnitude and how it can affect investment decisions. As I move forward through additional biases keep in mind that these DO apply to everyone.

The Biases

Most biases derive from heuristics which humans have developed to aid in the decision making process. Heuristics are nothing more than shortcuts, and people use heuristics thousands of times a day. An examination of the statistics of heuristics is impressive. A majority of the time these shortcut judgments are accurate and correct. However there are problems when using heuristics in an investment decision making process. The sections that follow will address cognitive mishaps that most investors make.

Narratives

Why are narratives or stories so impactful and easy to remember? The answer is relatively straight forward: stories summarize complex situation and tug at emotions, at least the remembered narratives do. Minds have evolved over thousands, maybe millions of years, and one of the most effective forms of learning is through storytelling. When parents want to teach a child about the negative impact of lying, what story do parents tell them? Pinocchio. Imagine the difficulty involved in explaining the emotional impact that lying has and its negative impact on both the liar and the one being lied to. It is much easier for a child to understand a story about a boy who lied, and his nose began to grow every time he told a lie.

This tale of a string puppet and his lying is an effective demon-stration about emotions and right and wrong. This holds true for adults as well. It is much easier to remember a story about the economy or stock market than it is for us to remember sta-tistics about it. The stronger the emotions that are tied to the story, the easier it is to retell and the easier it is remember.

Narratives are another heuristic that make sense of complex information. For example, the stock market. Clients expect an advisor to know why the market went up or down today and as long as I can use a story explaining why this happened they are content. They will talk to their neighbor and regurgitate the same story with ease. However the truth of the matter is advisors do not know precisely why the market fluctuated, but a believable story from a media talking head or an analyst for a big investment firm will be accepted as valid. The truth is advisors feel extremely nervous when they cannot explain things. That is why the standard Wall Street saying is, "The markets do not like uncertainty."

One way to counter this behavioral heuristic is to understand that it is acceptable to not know something, and it is a great virtue to admit absolute ignorance. Confucius said it best, "True wisdom is knowing what you don't know." This often gives investors a feeling of uneasiness, but it is critical for those who aspire to be successful investors. Most things about investing are not explainable such as why stocks that are nearly identical move in opposite directions, or why the stock market goes up one day and down the next. Society's members have an unquenchable thirst to make sense of surroundings instead of accepting the fact that such is not possible in every situation. Something to think about while reading the rest of this book. Suppose an investor owns General Electric, and to-day the stock price goes up by $1, tomorrow it goes down by $5, and the next day it goes up by $10. Financial emotions just took a rollercoaster ride. But consider this question. What could have possibly happened in GE's business that would cause the value of the company, this massive company, to fluctuate so much? Think about the answer to that question and keep it foremost in the mind while reading the rest of this chapter.

Anchoring

Studies have shown that people tend to anchor on numbers that are completely irrelevant to the task they are attempting. For example, if I randomly say "125" and hold up a jar full of peanuts and ask how many peanuts are in the jar. Many responses will be close to "125." This is called anchoring, and all are guilty of it.

I once read an article about how Warren Buffet determines the price he is willing to pay for a stock. He first reads the latest annual report and from there does his analysis to determine what he sees as the intrinsic value for the company. The key that most miss was what he said next. He never looks at the company's current market price before he does his analysis. This makes perfect sense, and anyone who studies behavioral finance understands exactly why he does this. He has effectively removed the temptation for his mind to anchor on a price. Now, behavioral finance has been practiced for some time, but Mr. Buffet has been investing over 50 years. I would think that it is safe to say that Mr. Buffet has been one step ahead of the game for quite some time.

Experiencing vs. Remembering

Advisors need to keep in mind what psychologists call the peak-end rule. Humans tend to judge their experiences whether good or bad not on the average of the experience but on how they felt at their peak and at or near the end of the experience. I know some advisors are reading this thinking,

"This explains so much about my clients." Advisors and investors know why some who have been investing for twenty years and have on average made six percent per year including the losses of 2008, can only remember the pain they felt when they suffered through that horrible year. They forget about how well they have done on average and lean on their peak emotional experiences. Daniel Kahneman (2011), observes that there are two different people living in the inside of each person: the experiencing self and the remembering self. He states that memories are constructed on our peak-end experience and very little is memory of what we actually experience as a whole.

The Paradox of Control

The **Paradox of Control** is the tendency for people to overestimate their ability to control events. For instance individuals sometimes feel a control over outcomes that they have demonstrated no influence over whatsoever. Investors are addicts for more and more information. Additional information tends to communicate control over the outcome. One study by O'Creevey, Nicholson, Soane, and Willman (2003) examined traders in the City of London's investment banks. They were all asked to use three computer keys as they watched a real-time graph similar to a stock chart. They had to use the computer keys to raise the value as high as possibly. They were also informed that the value showed random variations, but they might have some effect over the overall value by using the computer keys. The truth was that the computer keys had zero effect on the outcome and the traders' ratings of their success measured their susceptibility to the paradox of control. The score was compared to performance. The conclusion was quite startling. Those who were prone to the paradox of control scored significantly lower on analysis, risk management among other investment variables. They also earned significantly less. This behavior is constantly on display in the investing world. As investors gain more and more information on the economy, they believe they can make a reasonable assumption as to where the stock market is heading. They become confident in this information, maybe a little too confident.

There have been studies on this positive paradox that show people are motivated by this paradox and will be more persistent at tasks they have no control over if they believe they in fact have some control over the outcome. Because a bias is bad for investing does not mean it is bad for decision makers. Most biases are good for some types of decision making processes but detrimental to others.

The Paradox of Knowledge

The **Paradox of Knowledge and Paradox of Control** go hand in hand. The Paradox of Knowledge will likely give way to the Paradox of Control. The Paradox of Knowledge is the tendency for people to believe the more information they have, the more accurate their forecast will be. A paper titled, "The Illusion of Knowledge: When more information reduces accuracy and increases confidence," Hall et al., described an experiment where a group of participants were asked to predict the outcome of basketball games given specific statistics about the games. Half of the participants were given additional information which was the team's name. Knowledge of the names increased the confidence of the participants, and they believed improved their predictions. However the study found that the opposite actually occurred. The additional information decreased the accuracy of the participants because it simultaneously reduced their reliance on the actual statistics of the games. A real betting experiment concluded that the fans who knew the team's names actually earned less money than the fans who only had statistics. A great example of this is the movie Money Ball, starring Brad Pitt. This movie is based on the Oakland A's approach to recruiting players based on an analytical, evidence-based, sabermetric approach to assembling a competitive team when management was faced with limited financial resources. They analyzed statistics on a team level as opposed to individual mundane statistics such as a player's batting average. This is an important lesson for most investors. We are often biased towards companies that we know. The more a company appears in the news, the more we will be biased towards this company thinking we have knowledge regarding its future without regard for the statistics. If the media is pumping it up, it must be good.

What generally happens under the Paradox of Knowledge is investors become overconfident. Most investors believe that the more information they have, the better decisions they will make. Overconfidence is a bias all investors face. Reading annual reports and analyst reports, pulling together income statements and balance sheets may result in hundreds of pages of information about a company, yet if we do not know what to look for, we will never find it. Unfortunately, a majority of investors believe the more information they have, the better they are at making decision. Often times we have too much information and waste hours sifting through this data which often lends to overconfidence in stock selection and a paradox of knowledge.

A paper published in the Journal of Economic Psychology called "Harmful effects of seemingly helpful information on forecasts of stock earnings", Davis et al, brings to light the concepts of both Paradox of Knowledge and Overconfidence. Davis et al.'s study was conducted on MBA students taking advanced financial statement analysis. The only task was to forecast fourth-quarter earnings for different firms. Each firm's information was formatted in three different ways. The first included the baseline of the previous three quarters EPS, the stock price, and net revenue. The second way data was presented was with all the baseline data plus irrelevant information. The final way was with the baseline data plus relevant information which was believed to help increase the forecasting ability of the group. The results were astonishing. Each participant was presented the same company in three different formats, and the forecast error was highest in both the baseline plus irrelevant information AND relevant information. The forecast error was lowest among baseline information only. This shows that investors are overconfident as a result of the Paradox of Knowledge. The most surprising thing about this study is that it did not matter if information was relevant or not; the participant did better with less information. This is why it is important to pay attention only to information used to make a decision, all other information is irrelevant. I have mentored advisors, and when I asked them to show me what they analyzed in their decision making process, I cannot believe how much of their information was irrelevant to their actual decision. They will show me stock screens for every imaginable stock metric available, sector analysis for 168 different industries, and broad economic data, but when I ask about their strategy, they will say they are bottom-up, long-term, buy and hold investor. A bottom-up, buy and hold investor can eliminate nearly every other piece of information except the process and stock valuation metrics. An authentic bottom up and buy and hold and will not care about sector leaders or what the economy is currently doing. They are looking for the best, well run companies that they believe will continue to grow book value for years and years to come believing all the other information should be scrapped. Additional information does not help if it is not vital to the outcome of the analysis. It provides a dose of Overconfidence.

Before the subject of the Paradox of Control/Knowledge, there is another study that is relevant. I assume most have heard about, B.F. Skinner's "Superstition in the Pigeon." In this ex-

periment Skinner uses hungry pigeons to test for operant conditioning. Operant conditioning is a type of learning where an
individual's behavior is modified by the consequence of the behavior. Skinner placed the pigeons in cages with an automatic
feeder that would dispense food at fixed intervals. The food
will be dispensed without regard to the bird's behavior. The
results were amazing. Skinner wrote, "In six out of eight cases
the resulting responses were so clearly defined that two observers could agree perfectly in counting instances. One bird
was conditioned to turn counter-clockwise about the cage,
making two or three turns between reinforcements. Another
repeatedly thrust its head into one of the upper corners of the
cage." He goes on to describe the conditioned behavior of the
other birds and concluded that these birds suffered from the
Paradox of Control.

Hindsight Bias

For the last several years I have been keeping a "trade journal." In this journal is record of all my buy and sell decisions,
my thoughts on the economy, and other relevant investment
thoughts. When I analyze a stock and decide that I want to
add it to my portfolio, I write down the reason I made this decision, what fundamental data I used to arrive at the decision,
and so on. I do the same for my technical charts. When I decide to take a new position or add to an existing positon, I write
down the reason I am taking this action and the same is true
for selling a position. Journaling will help investors recognize
not only Hindsight bias but many other behavioral flaws.

Hindsight bias, also known as creeping determinism is a psychological tendency that people have, thinking that after an
event has occurred it was more predictable than it actually
was. Sometimes they even go as far as to believe they knew
the result was going to happen. You will often hear, "I knew
that was going to happen."

Hindsight bias has a major draw-back that I believe makes it one of the worst if not the worst bias. Hindsight bias prevents investors from recognizing mistakes and when warned of its dangers and susceptibility, fail to see it in themselves. Bruno Biasis and Martin Weber (2009) found in two separate studies that it did matter if inexperienced or experienced in forecasting, there is a high probability that investors experience at least some aspects of Hindsight bias. The students in the study were asked to forecast the price of certain assets for the next week within a 90% confidence interval. Once the students were told the results, they believed their forecasts were closer to the actual value than they actually were.

Hindsight bias is a simple concept yet it is likely the hardest to overcome. It is difficult to eliminate this bias by simply warning investors of it. However, Fischhoff in a 1982 paper believes that the bias can be reduced when individuals are asked to explain how events, which did not occur, could have occurred. One way to reduce hindsight bias as suggested by Harry Wallace and colleagues is to try to continually gain knowledge. They have found that having to work hard to gain knowledge causes people to lower their perceived level of past knowledge. A daily gain of knowledge and insight may reduce hindsight bias even if only slightly.

Confirmatory Bias

Also called Myside bias is the tendency to search for information or even interpret information that confirms individual beliefs or thoughts. Confirmatory bias is prevalent in how society is driven and divided. When meeting someone new for the first time and leaving the conversation with a feeling of friendship, participants experienced confirmatory bias. People tend to look for commonalities in almost everything. When meeting someone, people try to decide if there is a commonality. Rarely are two people best friends if they have different belief systems, such as an Atheist and a Christian. It can happen, but it is not a standard situation. This is why there are social norms and democrats and republican parties. Likeminded people tend to enjoy being around each other. When searching for a spouse, most look for common ground in beliefs and childhood experiences; however, that does not mean someone must be identical to another person in every way, but most do look for common ground.

The above example does a poor job of explaining confirmatory bias, so look at an example put forth by James Montier (2007).

> Consider the following situation: Four cards are laid out in front of you, and each card carries one alphanumeric symbol. The set comprises E, 4, K, 7. If I tell you that if a card has a vowel on one side, then it should have an even number on the other, which card(s) do you need to turn over to see if I am telling the truth?

Now think about it for a minute. Most people would choose E and 4. Montier goes on to explain the correct answer is E and 7. Only these two cards can prove whether the statement was true or not. If a person turns over the E and there is an odd number, the statement is false, and if turning over the 7 and there is a vowel, again the statement is false. However, turning over the 4 cannot prove the statement true or false; one can only confirm the statement but not prove the assertion. Why then choose the 4? We are all programmed to look for information that confirms opinions. As demonstrated the first example, when meeting someone who agrees with our opinions, participants feel validated and tend to want to be around those people. When someone disagrees, the tendency is to jump to the defense instead of listening and entertaining an idea that might change previously held conceptions. If two people agree in opinion and a third party disagrees, the two that are in agreement will automatically form an alliance against the third person without considering a need to change their own opinion.

This same bias affects decision making in regards to investing. Investing is not a science, as much as some would like to think it is; it is far from it. There are multiple "right" ways to invest money: invest in growth stocks or value stocks or even commodities, etc. So there are multiple ways of doing the same thing and still being successful. This industry is full of opinions. Confirmatory bias is extremely difficult to detect in such an opinionated environment. For example, an investor is considering an investment in XYZ stock and the investor believes that this stock is undervalued and a debate on the local media with two opposing views is being aired. One analyst says the stock is overvalued and gives a valid reason why, and the other analyst that says this stock is a buy and is only going higher; he too has a valid reason why. Which analyst is right? Most in this scenario would agree with the analyst that shares their opinion and completely disregard the other analyst. This is confirmatory bias.

How can this bias be minimized in investment decisions? Even though it is difficult to spot confirmatory bias, if an investment strategy includes all opposing information, it is possible to entertain at the least a different point of view. Montier states that if investors sit down with people who disagree and are unable to identify a logical flaw in their argument, there is a need to reconsider how tightly to hold to a point of view.

Self-Attribution Bias

This is another critical issue facing all investors. I call this the blame game. This is a heavy topic for most firms that attempt to pull together an investment committee to try and arrive at truth. It is difficult for investors to admit mistakes. They have an image to keep, especially the ones who are financial advisors. I have sat in conference rooms with financial advisors as they explained sub-par performance to their investment clients, and there are some wild excuses explaining the sub-par performance. However, I have never heard an advisor admit that it was lack of skill that caused the performance. Self-attribution bias is the tendency for people to try and find reasons to justify mistakes or behaviors. I call this the "we and I" bias. If involved in a team project and sitting in or listening to someone present a case, pay attention to the words. For example suppose a lead financial advisor is meeting with a client who has three winning investments and two investments that have lost money. More than likely if the poor performance involves self-esteem, self-attribution bias will rear its head. The conversation probably goes like this: "Well the reason the XYZ and ABC investments have done poorly WE believe is because the industry is suffering from over supply. However, I noticed early on when I decided to add these three particular investments that outperformed had a fabulous management team." Advisors tend to attribute good outcomes to skill and bad outcomes to bad luck. This however limits the ability to learn from mistakes.

I once read an article that said, "Don't Confuse Brains with a Bull Market." I read that title and it took a minute to sink in as to what it was trying to say. We all suffer from self-attribution bias to some degree, and this little phrase sums it up for most investors. When in a bull market and selected stocks become winners and the majority of a portfolio's positions are positive, there is a tendency to think this stock picking thing has been figured out. But when the market corrects a few percent and investors sell positions and buy some others and the bull market is still moving forward, this reinforces our self-attribution since the correction and the continuation of the bull market led investors to believe stocks were sold when necessary to sell and bought even better securities because once again the majority of investing positions were positive. As this little cycle continues to evolve during a bull market, some investors tend to become overconfident in their abilities, letting their guard down so to speak, and self-attribution takes over and many investors believe they are in control of the investment markets. On the other hand, if a major bear market takes hold, and investors sell on the first dip to take "better" positions just as during the entire bull market, but this time the market breaks down. Since generally a bear market is harsher but briefer than a bull market, there is a tendency to think that no one missed the correction, and since most major sell offs are associated with major events, some believe it was bad luck not lack of skill as the reason for not realizing the market has completely changed course. This is where keeping a trade journal comes in to play. Investing and writing down the reasons for making specific decisions and monitoring the decision making process through an entire market cycle can potentially identify this bias as well as where there was a display of actual skill and where it was inherently luck. Please notice that several of these biases overlap or reinforce one or the other. Self-attribution bias reinforces investor overconfidence, and since these two behaviors reinforce each other, it does the investor an even greater injustice in that it forfeits the investor the ability to learn from mistakes since mistakes are blamed on bad luck or things beyond their control.

ADHD Bias

I believe every child who has ever been diagnosed with Attention Deficit Hyperactivity Disorder (ADHD) grew up to work in the financial industry. It seems that the more information investors have and the faster that information is received, the more myopic we become. Montier (2007) states that in the 1950's investors held investment positions for seven to eight years whereas today investors tend to hold a stock for only eleven months. With the advent of the internet and nearly instantaneous data, investors have become increasingly myopic in investment time horizons. Imagine day trading in the 1950's in the pits on the actual exchanges. As computers came online and real-time stock quotes became the norm, investors have been bombarded with relative performance and information overload. Attention spans have shrunk from years to days, and performance data is available on any smart phone. What has this done to the investment industry? Most portfolio managers have increasingly shortened investment holding periods to avoid underperforming on a short-term basis. In the portfolio management industry, the portfolio manager is paid a fee on assets-under-management, which is generally fixed. If managers underperform a benchmark, impatient investors will move money away from those advisors and to a money manager who has beat a benchmark over the same period. Investors are often short sighted and tend to chase performance. I believe the main cause of this bias to the fact that investors still "benchmark" returns on a relative basis as opposed to evaluating performance on an absolute basis. This ADHD bias is a trickle up distortion of investor behavior. Investors now have more information, which gives them more confidence which leads to overconfidence in their ability to invest and make wise investment decisions. This demand for short-term performance is infused in portfolio managers' minds since underperformance this quarter may result in lost assets even if the same managers have outperformed over the last three years. The vast majority of portfolio managers are going to do what investors demand even if it is not in the best interest of the investor over the long-term.

One study conducted by Montier (2007) was to create a universe of 100 imaginary mutual fund managers, each with a 0.5 information ratio. The information ratio can be broken down into a 3% alpha and a 6% tracking error which by any standard is a good track record over a long-term horizon. He back-tested the managers performance for 50 years and arrived at some interesting facts. First, almost one in three underperformed the benchmark every single year. Dissecting the information further, he discovered that on average each manager spent approximately fifteen years underperforming the benchmark with a minimum of nine years. Montier noticed that with a 3% alpha, three year underperformance was actually normal. He concluded that:

> Despite the managers having a high alpha and information ratio, it wouldn't have been enough to prevent almost every one of the fund managers from being fired by their clients at some point over the 50 years.

This is a topic that is difficult for advisors to explain to a client. When a client is reviewing an investment statement on a monthly basis, shock is likely. Any investment strategy or discipline falls out of favor from time to time. When an investor has a mind set on relative instead absolute returns, there can be a loss of sight of the almost scientific proof: on occasion the soundest investment strategy will underperform relative to a specific benchmark. If investors and even advisors can begin to focus attention on absolute returns rather than relative returns, all may look at investing in a different light and not be reactive in decisions and change investment strategies and advisors. Most investors need to understand that relative returns, the ones that are constantly being touted in the media and of which all money managers are compared, are absolutely useless to a retired investor living off a portfolio. It does the retired investor no good to look at an annual return and see a 25% loss and be excited about outperforming a benchmark that has fallen 30%; they are still down 25%.

Empathy Gap

This next topic, the empathy gap will tie this information together. This is the section to apply what has been learned. All
have the capability of gaining knowledge or learning new
things, but it is in the application of this new found information that actually creates knowledge.

An investor's empathy gap is by far the hardest to detect without a trade journal. An empathy gap is a cognitive bias in
which a person underestimates the influences of visceral
drives and instead attributes behavior primarily to other, non-
visceral factors. This means that investors underestimate
emotions when in a hot state versus a cold state. This is prevalent in investors more often than any other bias. For example
when an investor is going to sell ABC stock if the price hits a
certain dollar amount or misses its earnings estimates, but
when this happens, the investor does not sell and uses the excuse that views have changed. This is an empathy gap. Maybe
a better example is thirst. After drinking three glasses of water, it is difficult to imagine being thirsty, but if sitting in the
desert without water dying of thirst, it is not possible to imagine what it would be like not to be thirsty. An empathy gap is
the difference between feeling and thinking, and investors often cannot tell the difference.

Empathy gaps are generally justified with an excuse. Investors
are now dealing with how they feel and how they think they
will feel when the moment arrives. It is easy for an investor to
believe they would sell a stock if it misses earnings, but when
the time comes and the company misses earnings and the stock
price plummets 10% overnight, the tendency is to try and justify not taking the 10% loss. I believe investment journaling
and seeing these emotionally caused reactions in the heat of
the moment will allow analysis of these emotions and possibly
allow an investor to "learn" how to feel when the time actual
comes to implement an investment strategy.

Loss Aversion

Most advisors have explained the term "risk aversion" to clients and most are fairly comfortable with the term. In MPT and the EMH theory, risk aversion is a measure of volatility. If two investments have the same expected return but one is less volatile than the other, a rational investor is supposed to pick the less volatile or less risky investment, right? Maybe. If we look at investing from the perspective that we have an opportunity for gain but with this opportunity comes a risk of loss of part or all of our money, investors and advisors may be less likely to make rational investing decisions. Kahneman poses a question for all investors to consider: if offered the choice to gamble on a coin toss where the outcome is the loss of $100 if the coin lands on tails, but a win of $150 if the coin lands on heads. Who would take the gamble? Rational investors would do the statistics and discover the outcome based on probabilities is positive. So a rational investor would take the gamble every time. However, several experiments have concluded that most investors have a loss aversion ratio of about 2-to-1. This means that our emotions are twice as strong regarding a loss as they are for an equal size gain. So for the above experiment we would need $200 to entice us to consider taking the bet. Loss aversion and Risk Aversion are not the same thin

Mental Accounting

There have been several studies conducted regarding why investors tend to sell winners and keep losers, which is called the Disposition Effect. The disposition effect and metal accounting are closely linked. Why does the disposition effect exist? An understanding of mental accounting is necessary and can be described relatively easy with an example. Suppose an investor's car breaks down and there is a need to sell a stock from a portfolio in order to cover the cost of $2,000. Let us assume one stock, ABC, could be sold for a gain of $2,000, while XYZ could be sold for a loss of $2,000. Which stock should be sold to cover repair expenses? Mental accounting does that; it allows us to keep score mentally. It is the ability to exercise self-control but at other times it is a nuisance. A rational investor would sell the loser in the above example, taking the loss. This is rational since we know losses are favored taxably in the United States and winners tend to keep on winning. However, most humans and for that matter emotional decision makers are keeping score mentally and do not want to feel the pain of a loss but want to feel the reward of an accomplishment. Financial advisors should understand why it is so hard to communicate with clients regarding decisions on which stocks to sell or decisions regarding how to manage a client's portfolio. Most investors are keeping track of every position in their mind, and each time an advisor sales a loser it causes them pain, which in turn likely results in a tongue lashing over the phone. An advisor must explain this concept to clients for not only their mental health but their financial health as well. A rational investor would take a more comprehensive overview of the entire portfolio and decide which stock to sell, not based on gains or loses but rather based on which stock was likely to do poorly in the future. It would be a good practice to always step back and ask, "Would I make this decision if I were truly rational?" Only then will advisors or investors cease making rash decisions in the heat of the moment.

Behavioral Finance fills in many gaps that are left open in the theory of efficient markets. It is however not the be all end all of financial theory. Humans may behave irrationally in certain situations, but the millions of people investing in the markets are not all irrational and some do make rational investing decision while others are lucky. Minds have evolved over millions of years to protect from danger and increase the probability for survival. At the same time brains have evolved in such a way that at times humans are at odds with rational decision making. This is much like going to the zoo and visiting the snake exhibit. Viewers inch closer and closer to the glass cages and even ignore the sign stating not to tap on the glass when suddenly the snake strikes. Most will jump back instantly without even thinking. Was that a rational decision or an automatic decision based on millions of years of evolution that informs to move when danger strikes? Even if we are certain that there is no need to jump back because that would be irrational, it is difficult to contain emotional decisions even when that decision is irrational. This example makes the case for how hard it is to control emotions. Hopefully investors will be able to recognize and minimize emotional decisions during investing, and a financial advisor will be able to steer clients toward understanding that it is often emotions that are detrimental to financial health not the strategy.

[3]

The Choice Is Up to the Investor

In the previous chapters I explained the two main views on market efficiency. The EMH theory will lead to investing passively. Behavioral finance will lead toward active management in order to take advantage of market inefficiencies. Please, notice the continued use of the word "believe" and a reluctance to endorse one way as correct and the other way as incorrect.

There are two schools of thought on this subject. Rene Descartes believed that understanding a subject and believing in it are two separate tasks. This is how humans would like to think minds worked: when presented with new information or new ideas, evaluate the idea before deciding to believe in the idea. Another philosopher, Benedict Spinoza argued we must first believe in the idea before understanding. This is somewhat scary. When presented with new information or a new concept or idea, most tend to believe it is true first therefore giving the mind the ability to process and understand the information, and then decide if in fact it is true. This second step is only completed with effort: most don't seek to disprove ideas unless the new information that is presented contradicts their current beliefs. It is nearly impossible to change minds unless it is scientifically proven which when referring to beliefs is rarely possible. For example a Christian will generally dismiss the ideas presented to them by atheist that there is no God. They do not believe the new information therefore cannot understand it. A better example is a Christian presented with scientific information about the creation of the universe. They do not believe it and therefore do not understand it. This is an example of two opposing beliefs systems that are equally difficult to prove beyond a doubt that one is true and the other is false. It comes down to beliefs. It is difficult to change a long held belief and to have an open mind. When individuals experience new information, the presenter knows the data probably goes against current beliefs. They say, "Now, keep an open mind when I present this information." However, an authentic open mind takes considerable effort. I am personally a Christian and have struggled with keeping an open mind when presented with information that does not necessarily contradict my faith but presents an alternative hypothesis from what I hold as true.

I share this because investors must believe in their investment philosophy or it is impossible to understand what is happening within their portfolio. If an investor believes it is impossible to beat the market by managing actively, and the investment manager he has chosen (highly unlikely they would choose this type of manager) to invest their assets is an active manager, they would be upset every time their portfolio underperforms its benchmark without taking into consideration when it outperforms during a bear market. That is why during times of underperformance many investors change strategies generally at the worst possible times. Since too many tend to believe first and ask questions later, it is easy to see why some change minds. If a portfolio is underperforming and investors or advisors are presented with information about a new strategy that is doing well in the current environment, both believe first and change strategies; however, only during the next period of underperformance do either ask questions. Keeping an open mind is critical to success, but it is critical to change the way we process information: believe first and ask questions later, or ask questions first and believe later.

So, which type of investment philosophy is the most advantageous? As a portfolio manager it is obvious I take the side of active management and believe behavioral biases are present in the financial markets which create inefficiencies. However, I will be the first to say that active management is not the only way to be successful. It is all about expectations. A passive investor cannot expect to avoid the next financial crisis or the next bear market. Another bear market like the one currently in control and that began in 2001 is still in effect in 2015. Only time will tell whether the all-time highs of 2015 will hold. An investor must be prepared for negative returns on an inflation adjust basis for a decade or more. An active investor cannot expect to outperform the market every year. It has not happened and will probably never happen. Active investors must be prepared for underperformance, when the market goes up 20% but their portfolio only does 5%. These are all expectations that are hard to deal with when they arise.

When investors and financial advisors ask what I personally believe, I tend to surprise them when I say both, and they react with a look of disapproval because it appears I have contradicted my own teachings. Investing for most people is black and white, but for me it is grey. There is a place for both active and passive investing. I manage money in an active way. I believe that the investment markets are MOSTLY efficient; however, there are times when the markets are inefficient due to the irrational behavior of human investors. During the market bottom in early 2009, a large number of companies traded at historically low multiples and some traded below liquidation value. This presented an opportunity that was advantageous to smart money. During this time the markets were irrational and inefficient. The same holds true during market exuberance in 1999 and 2000.

This concept of utilizing both active and passive investing was developed by Fischer Black and Jack Treynor (1973). The concept is known as the Treynor/Black Model. This model assumes that most securities are efficiently priced, but there are a limited number of securities that are inefficiently priced. This mathematical model states that the optimal portfolio consists of two parts. First a passively invested indexed portfolio that contains all securities in the market place and secondly, an active portfolio that contains the securities that are mispriced. In the active portfolio the weight of each stock is proportional to the alpha value divided by the variance of the residual risk. This model is simple in concept but fairly difficult for the average investor to follow strictly based on their own model. It is a hybrid model that considers both arguments. As mentioned in the introduction, some people may believe in active management but are not willing to put in the time to do necessary homework in order to manage an active investment portfolio. They may, and most do, hire a professional money manager to manage their assets actively while others choose to invest for themselves in a passive strategy. Some decide to loosely follow the Treynor/Black model in that they split their portfolios in to separate areas of active and passive strategies. They may purchase index funds that track a specific benchmark and invest the other portion in an active strategy such as dividend paying blue-chip stocks they believe to be trading at or below intrinsic value. Once again there is no magic way to invest a portfolio that will beat benchmarks every year and never have a down year. They simply do not exist. Recently, the world's greatest investor has suffered his worst period of underperformance since he began managing money more than 50 years ago. That is right. Warren Buffet has underperformed his benchmark for the last five years according to his preferred measure of book value performance. This does not mean his strategy no longer works; it means it is out of favor in the current investment environment. Every active investor will suffer such disappointments in an investment career, but the key to investment success is to stick with a strategy and see it through.

It is now time to decide how to manage an investment portfolio. Is success within investing actively, passively, or a mixture of both? A completely passive investor may save time by skipping to the chapter on passive investment management and skipping the chapters on fundamental and technical analysis. If an investor believes a portion of an investment is best managed in an active manner, proceed to part two and discover examples of valuation models. If an investor is considering hiring a money manager, read the next part of this book in order to understand how an investment manager determines the value of a company.

PART II

Valuation

Reading this introduction should pique interest in the idea that stock prices can vary from their intrinsic value and therefore create an opportunity for profit. This is related to the Black Jack analogy from the introduction that is equivalent to knowing which table is hot. A card counter can count cards on any Black Jack table, but the difference between success and failure lies in knowing which table to count cards on. In order to succeed in identifying companies that are trading below intrinsic value, an investor needs to first transition to the mind set of an analyst. The chapter on Efficient Market Hypothesis proposed that fundamental valuation is doomed to fail since valuation uses publically available information and thus should already be priced into the stock. Only analysts who have a unique insight that differs from the consensus can determine real value. This means that valuation is much more difficult than finding well run companies that appear to have a bright future, since many other analysts have already identified these well run companies and this is reflected in their stock price. This means an investor that only identifies well run companies that have a bright future will likely pay too high a price. The key to successful valuation techniques is not discovering what is already

discovered but using specific techniques to arrive at a valuation that differs from consensus. More about this when we discuss the Capital Asset Pricing Model.

I believe that valuation is the most critical step in the investment process. The public, including advisors, are bombarded
daily by market news and myopic investment advice and often
forget that this information may or may not be relevant to the
future value of the firm. As explained in the chapter on behavioral finance, there is a tendency to be myopic by nature and
investors are often tricked into making decision based on noise
rather than fundamental data. Ben Graham once said, "The
risk of paying too high a price for good quality stocks – while a
real one – is not the chief hazard confronting the average buyer
of securities. Observation over many years has taught us that
the chief losses to investors come from the purchase of low
quality securities at times of favorable business conditions."

Suppose a company earned $1.00 for every share it had out-
standing and that there were 1 million shares outstanding.
This would mean that the company today is worth $1 million.
Now let us assume the company grows earnings per share
(EPS) by 10% per year and will continue to do so for the next
five years. At the end of the fifth year, the company will distribute all its earnings to its shareholders. The future value of
the company's earnings at the end of five years would be
$1.61[1.00 * (1.10)^5]$

So in this hypothetical world, $1,000,000 today would grow
to $1,610,000 in five years, a 61% return. This makes investing
sound simple and straightforward. If the assumptions were
true and the company did earn the forecasted 10% on its EPS,
anyone would give one dollar today to receive $1.61 in five
years. Another dimension to this scenario is to assume there
are twenty million investors who want to buy this stock. The
current owners of the stock are unlikely to sell any shares for

$1.00 today, because they can hold the stock for five years and receive $1.61. Society knows that in the real world no one can predict if a company will grow at 10% per year, and most companies will not distribute 100% of their earnings. So the question is, how much to pay today for this company's future earnings of $1.61? Refer to the chapter on EMH and behavioral finance and this situation will make more sense. If all information is known, which means certain knowledge that the company will earn 10% on its earnings and will pay out all earnings in five years, investors will refuse to pay more than $1.61 per share. In fact, most investors will not pay $1.61 today to receive $1.61 in the future. According to EMH the stock price today is $1.61 because all information is known and priced into the stock which would eliminate the ability to pay less than intrinsic value for a stock.

Add another dimension to this scenario and assume that, as in the real world, future earnings cannot be known for certain. What would an investor be willing to pay today for this stock? What if the stock can earn 20%, or even 30% per year on its earnings for the next five years, might this change the price an investor would pay? Of course it would. This is why behavioral finance is so important, and why reading this chapter is important. Since it is all the investor's decisions that make up the market price, from now on I will refer to all investors as "the market." If all investors believe the company will earn the 10% on earnings as in the first example, the market price would be $1.61. However, after doing homework, the investor believes the company will actually grow its earnings per share at 20% per year for the five years before distributing them. This would value the company at $2.48. Would an investor pay $1.61 today, (the market's value at a 10% growth of EPS) even though earnings today are only $1.00, if the earnings will be $2.48 in five years? Of course! The Efficient Market Hypothesis price would be the $1.61, the price that the market believes contains all available information. The $2.48 price is the price that differs from the consensus and is where valuation adds value.

At the root of valuation is the principle that a company is worth all its future cash flows discounted back to the present at the appropriate discount rate to arrive at a value today that all future cash flows would be worth. The key assumption for successful valuation of individual companies is that the market price that a company is currently on sale for can be different than the company's intrinsic value. Intrinsic value is a hypothetical value. It is the value obtained when there is a complete understanding of every characteristic of a company. The intrinsic value formed from the valuation is $2.48 while the market price is $1.61. The estimated intrinsic value represents the real or true value of a stock to the investor who estimated the intrinsic value.

The key to successfully estimate a company's intrinsic value is to have accurate forecast and use an appropriate valuation model. Later in this chapter is an exploration of different valuation models and the pros and cons of each. The hardest component of stock valuation is that the majority of the inputs of a valuation model are estimates. It is the quality of these estimates that make or break the success of an active investor. For an investor to be consistently successful, expectations must differ from the market's consensus and on average be correct. What is even more disheartening is that not only do investors have to go against the crowd, which has been shown to cause real pain in behavioral studies, (Eisenberger and Lieberman 2004), but even if an investor is correct and takes into consideration that all risks and forecasts are spot-on, success is not guaranteed. There are several reasons for this. One is the investor's time-horizon may not be long enough for the assumed mispricing to converge to the estimated intrinsic value. Sometimes market corrections can change the perceived mis-

pricing and overall investment landscape causing these temporary conditions to be more or less permanent as far as the
investor is concerned.

Valuation Concepts

Abasic understanding of valuation was given in the previous section. Let me now give an overview of a very broad three step process to valuation. Before crunching numbers and forecasting sales and earnings for a company it is critical to **understand the business being considered as an investment**. What is the company's competitive advantage? How does the company compare to other competitors within the same industry? It is at this stage of the valuation process the prudent investor weeds out the majority of companies and focuses on the leaders within an industry or sector. A checklist for this part of the analysis would be Porter's Five Forces[1]. Michael Porter's Five Forces is a framework used to determine the level of competition within an industry. The Five Forces are:

1. *Threat of new entrants.* How competitive is the industry in which the company operates? If the industry is difficult to enter by competitors, the company can earn higher profits. Several factors inhibit competitors from entering an industry such as high fixed cost and

---

[1] Porter, M.E. (March–April 1979). "How Competitive Forces Shape Strategy." *Harvard Business Review*

initial investment or economies of scale or maybe patent protection. If however the industry is easy to enter, competition will be high and profitability will be lower.

2. **Threat of substitutes.** Are there any other products or services that can be substituted for the company's products or services under analysis? Substitutes that are lower priced could potentially attract a significant proportion of market volume from the company under analysis. Think about Coke Cola and Pepsi.

3. *Bargaining power of customers.* Few customers in an industry generally have the ability to influence the price of a product or service if they buy in large volumes or if switching to an alternative product is relatively simple and will not cost too much.

4. *Bargaining power of suppliers.* If suppliers of raw materials or other inputs are large and few in number, they tend of have the upper hand on the cost of the end product. There could be no substitutes for a particular input which would also hurt the company's ability to bargain for lower cost on raw materials.

5. *Competitive rivalry between existing companies.* If an industry is highly competitive, profit margins tend to be lower for all companies as each company within the industry cuts prices to gain market share in an environment with limited differentiation. An example would be a gas station. Most people will go wherever they can get a gallon of gas for the lowest cost.

Understanding a company's business model and strategy is extremely important. Not only is it a good idea to study each of Porter's five forces, but it is important to study the company's financial history by analyzing income statements, balance sheets, and cash flow statements as well as a company's annual report. When following a company for investment purposes, this phase of the valuation process is normally done only once or until a full understanding of the business is accom-plished. Only occasionally is there a need to review the indus-try as a whole to determine if trends have begun to change.

Now is a good time to determine the type of active investment style that will be applied to an investment strategy. There are two broad investment styles used in active investment man-agement: top-down and bottom-up investing. Top-down inves-tors take a macro look at economic conditions to determine which sectors or industries to begin focusing their research. A bottom-up investor will generally start at the individual com-pany level determining which company is undervalued based on a valuation method or model without regard to the com-pany's relative value among other companies within a sector or as to the direction of the overall economy. Either approach attempts to arrive at companies that are priced below their in-trinsic value, so it is a personal decision as to which style an investor follows.

Next is forecasting of sales, earnings, dividends, and other fi-nancial performance metrics. This step's results will be where the inputs for the valuation models come from, and will be dis-cussed later. Here the investor uses a top-down or bottom-up approach as well. Bottom-up forecasting uses the same con-cept as bottom-up investing. It starts at the company level. All three financial statements will need to be forecast in order to have a complete picture of the company's operations. For example, analyst often start a forecast with the income state-ment and in particular revenue. In a bottom-up approach, starting at the company level, analyst utilize a simple time se-ries regression model. Quantitative analysis is beyond the scope of this book though basic quantitative methods can eas-ily be performed using Excel. An analyst can enter ten years of revenue for a company and use the TREND function within Excel to draw a trend line. In this context an analyst would be projecting current growth rates into the future assuming past

growth rates would continue. This is the simplest of the methods for forecasting. A top-down approach may start with domestic or global Gross Domestic Product (GDP). If an analyst
uses global GDP, there is a need to decide by how much, either
faster or slower, the company would grow in relation to GDP.
So for example if Caterpillar Inc.'s (CAT) revenue tends to
grow at a 10% premium to GDP, when GDP is 4% CAT's revenue should increase by 14%. Regression analysis can also be
used here. With a top-down approach there are many more
variables that need to be forecast, and with the number of forecast increasing, the number of forecast errors are likely to increase as well. There are many more ways to forecast company
financial statements, and this explanation does not even
scratch the surface. Reading *Quantitative Investment Analysis by Defusco, McLeaven, Pinto, and Runkle* should provide a
complete understanding of quantitative methods. There are
numerous ways of forecasting and the most important element
is being comfortable and fully understanding the results of the
forecast.

The third step is to determine which valuation model to use,
which depends on the type of company being evaluated, the
company's financial characteristics, and whether the company
pays dividends. The two main types of valuation models are
absolute valuation models and relative valuation models.
Some analyst use both types of models and some are more comfortable using one over the other.

An absolute valuation model seeks to find the true value of the
company under analysis or its intrinsic value. This allows a
direct comparison with the company's current market price.
Absolute valuation models are used to arrive at price targets.
The most common type of absolute valuation models are present value models and are often referred to as discounted cash
flow models. The discounted cash flow models will be an ap-

propriate area to spend the majority of time as this incorporates financial theory concepts. Most are likely familiar with the time value of money so when hearing discounted cash flows or the present value of future cash flow, it is easy to understand exactly what is being discussed. For those who are not familiar with the concepts and application of the time value of money, stop here and mark this page, study the time value of money principles and return to finish this section on valuation models. A basic example of a present value calculation is as follows:

If an investor is certain to receive $1,000 in five years, what is it worth today if the prevailing interest rate is 5%? The future value (FV) is $1,000. The interest rate (r) is 5%, and the time (n) is five years. To calculate the present value (PV) of $1,000 to be received in five years is:

$$PV = \frac{FV}{(1+r)^5} = \frac{1000}{1.05^5} = \$753.53$$

Financial theory suggests a company is worth the present value of all future cash flows. This is a simple concept that is likely true. The difficult part is first forecasting the future cash flows of a company and determining the appropriate discount rate (interest rate) to use that accurately depicts future as well as present required rates of return. Some of the more common methods for determining appropriate rates of return will be explained later. Cash flows come in many different forms. Some analysts prefer to use dividends as the cash flow metric for valuation purposes since these are the cash flows that shareholders actually receive. If however a company does not pay a dividend, free cash flows are often a cash flow of choice. Even if a company pays a dividend and it is not stable, analysts may prefer to use free cash flows. Free cash flows are the cash flows remaining after paying debt and taxes. Previewing the differ-ent valuation models will provide more specifics as to how to arrive at the cash flow being used in the valuation model.

Another commonly used valuation model is the relative valua-tion model. This type of model estimates an asset's value rel-ative to that of another asset. The idea behind relative valuation is that companies in similar industries should trade for similar prices. The most common way this is accomplished is by using price multiples such as price-to-earnings or price-to-sales to compare the target company with the company's peers or even a benchmark. If company XYZ trades for ten times its earnings or has a P/E ratio of 10 and the median value for the P/E of all the companies that share the same industry is 15, the target company would be undervalued based solely on relative value. Some analysts use individual company com-parisons when deciding between two or more companies. Rel-ative valuation is the easiest to perform; however, it can be misleading. For example if one company has a P/E of 20 and the median P/E for the industry group is 10, it would appear that this company is expensive when compared to the industry; however, the target company could also be growing at twice the rate as the industry or have a differentiating product that would justify the higher ratio. This shows that investors or analysts cannot blindly follow a valuation but must strive to truly understand the results and the reasons behind the re-sults.

The underlying component for a sound and proper invest-ment decision is the required rate of return. Given the riski-ness of an asset, the required return is the minimum level of expected return that an investor requires in order to consider investing in the asset. There are several ways to measure the required rate of return using financial theory such as the widely known Capital Asset Pricing Model (CAPM). If inves-

tors' required return is less than their expected return assumptions, the stock is considered undervalued and vice versa
for overvalued. It is from the required and expected return
that the term "expected alpha" is born. Expected return minus
the required return is equal to the expected alpha from investing in the stock. Let us dig deeper into the determining factors
that make up the required rate of return.

Equity Risk Premium & Risk-Free Rate of Return

Prior to estimating the required rate of return it is necessary
to understand another input called the equity risk premium.
This is a relatively easy to understand concept, but the estimation of the equity risk premium can be challenging. If there is
a choice of investing money in a risk free asset such as U.S.
Treasury bonds or an individual stock, which is the most prudent choice? If the interest rate on the risk free bond was 5%
and the expected return on a stock was 5%, a risk adverse investor would choose the guaranteed bond. In all further calculations and assumptions regarding the risk-free asset or rate
of return, it will be assumed a time horizon equivalent government bond is used. If investing in Japanese companies, use
the rate of return on Japanese government bonds. A rational
investor would not be willing to take on risk without receiving
additional reward in the form of added returns. So the equity
risk premium is the return premium an investor requires in
order to hold a stock over a risk free asset. Here is another
concept to estimate. Like the required rate of return, the equity premium is an expectation about the future. There are
several ways to arrive at an equity risk premium. History data
can be used to forecast future risk premiums. A popular way
of doing this is to calculate the average return on a market
such as the S&P 500 and subtract the average return on government bonds over the same time period. This will give an
average risk premium that should hold on average, but just as

the market moves above and below its average so can the eq-uity risk premium. This can, on occasion, cause an analyst to over shoot or undershoot an estimate. There are several addi-tional ways to calculate the equity risk premium. Another very popular method of calculating the equity risk premium is to use the Gordon Growth Model Estimates which is based on the Gordon Growth model for estimating the value of stock which will be discussed in a later chapter. To utilize the Gordon Growth model to estimate the equity risk premium, an inves-tor or analyst needs the dividend yield for the relevant market index, the long-term earnings growth rate for the index, and the long-term government bond yield. The equity risk pre-mium is calculated by adding the dividend yield to the long-term earnings growth rate and subtracting the government bond yield. The last method is a macroeconomic model used by Chen (2003), et al. for estimating the equity risk premium. This method is based on overall economic growth rates and rates of inflation as well as expected yield from equity markets. The formula for this method is:

{[(1+expected inflation) * (1+expected earnings growth for the market) * (1+expected growth in P/E) – 1] + expected yield from the markets} – expected risk-free bond government bond returns

The above inputs are all in decimal form based on growth percentages. With a general understanding of the equity risk premium, investors can use this input to arrive at the required rate of return for valuation purposes.

The Capital Asset Pricing Model

The Capital Asset Pricing Model (CAPM) builds on Harry Markowitz's (1952) model of portfolio choice. The CAPM is the required rate of return on an asset in equilibrium. Kahn and Grinold (1999) call this the consensus return since it is what the market is expecting and requiring at the moment. CAPM also puts the burden of proof on an active manager since CAPM basically states that the consensus returns are a less risky investment than active management.

The CAPM attempts to determine the expected or required rate of return based on the sensitivity of the individual stock or portfolio compared to the market. This sensitivity is a form of market risk and must not be confused with total risk as measured by standard deviation. Standard deviation measures both systematic and unsystematic risk, while the CAPM utilizes only systematic risk and is measured by beta. Beta is calculated by taking the covariance between the stock and the market (such as S&P 500) and dividing it by the variance of the market.

$$\beta_p = \frac{Cov(p, m)}{\sigma_m^2}$$

Where:
$Cov(p, m)$= Covariance between portfolio and the market
σ_m^2= Variance of the Market
β_p= Beta of Portfolio

Covariance and variance will be discussed further in the chapter on portfolio management. Beta measures the sensitivity of the stock to that of the overall market. So assume a stock has a beta of two. This means that if the market goes up by 1%, this stock should go up twice as much, so it should go up 2%. The same is true for the downside. Studies have shown that over time beta converges to one. Blume (1971) introduced a formula that would allow an investor to make forward looking estimates based on historical beta estimates. The formula is:

Forward Looking Beta = (2/3)(Historical Beta) + (1/3)(1.0)

This sensitivity when combined with the expected return of the market and the risk-free rate will give the expected return on the stock. The CAPM calculation is present below.

$$E(r)_p = r_f + \beta_p(r_m - r_f)$$

Where:
$E(r)_p$ = Expected Return of a Portfolio
r_f = Risk-Free Rate of Return
β_p = Beta of the Portfolio
r_m = Return on the Market

The CAPM is one of the most fundamental concepts in investment theory. It is important to understand this concept as it will help investors develop and apply adaptations in order to value securities; however, Eugene Fama and Kenneth French (2004) stated the following:

> The attraction of the CAPM is that it offers powerful and intuitively pleasing predictions about how to measure risk and the relation between expected return and risk. Unfortunately, the empirical record of the model is poor – poor enough to invalidate the way it is used in applications. The CAPM's empirical problems may reflect theoretical failings, the result of many simplifying assumptions.

More on this can be found in the paper titled "The Capital Asset Pricing Model: Theory and Evidence."

The CAPM may not provide the best expected return, but it does provide a market consensus return. Multifactor models have taken precedence over the single risk premium concept. Multifactor models address different underlying factors that contribute to investment returns. For example arbitrage pricing theory (APT) add additional risk measures to the equation as well as betas. Most analysts and professional money managers have created proprietary risk factor models that harness the explanatory power of expected returns for which they are interested. The most popular non-proprietary multifactor model is the Fama-French multi-factor model (FFM)[2]. The FFM shares the market risk premium factor with the CAPM but adds two other factors to the equations. One is a market capitalization factor that takes the difference between three small capitalization portfolios and three large capitalization portfolios. This factor gives a return premium for small capitalization. The other factor is a value premium measured by book-to-market. Two high book-to-market portfolios are subtracted from two low book-to-market portfolios to obtain a value return premium. Thus, the FFM expected return is calculated as:

$$Rr_i = R_f + \beta_i^{mkt}(RMRF) + \beta_i^{size}(SMB) + \beta_i^{value}(HML)$$

Where:
Rr_i = *expected return*
β^{mkt} = *Beta sensitivity of stock to market*
β^{size} = *Beta sensitivity of stock to size*
β^{value} = *Beta sensitivity of stock to value*
RMRF = Market risk premium
SMB = Small capitalization premium

---

[2] Fama, E. F.; French, K. R. (1993). "Common risk factors in the returns on stocks and bonds." *Journal of Financial Economics* **33**: 3

HML = Value premium

There are many more formulas and theories regarding calcu-lating and estimating a required rate of return such as the bond yield plus risk premium and macroeconomic and statisti-cal multifactor models. The point is to have a basic under-standing of required return estimation and the underlying assumptions. The rational for going over these required return estimates is to clarify the importance this rate plays in calcu-lating the present value of future cash flows which is the root of equity valuation.

For the remainder of this book, unless otherwise specified, when referring to the required rate of return, assume that it was derived from the CAPM equation.

[5]

Present Value Models

It is important to remember that investing in stocks represents ownership of a business. Many times investors put this fundamental definition in the back of their minds as they attempt to buy and sell stocks trying to make a quick buck. There is nothing wrong with trading, but trading is not investing. If taking a fundamental approach to stock investing, the main goal is to find businesses to own and determine the price to pay to take an ownership role within the business. This also does not mean an owner must hold on to a company for long periods of time though that is the long term goal. Sometimes businesses fall out of favor or are unable to continue to grow, and as a stock owner it is easier to sell the stock on the open market than it would be to sell an entire business. Stock owners are entitled to the cash flows that this company generates as well as all future cash flows. That is the reason to invest today: the hopes of increased future cash flows. As previously discussed, the present value of all expected future cash flows represents the intrinsic value of a company. The goal is to determine what those future cash flows are worth today and compare that price with the price the market is telling investors it is worth. The concept of discounted cash flow models is relatively simple, and as with an-ything that uses forecasts investors are prone to errors in judg-ment. There are a few basic steps in performing discounted cash flow (DCF) analysis such as choosing the type of DCF model that best represents the future cash flows. There are Dividend Discount models, Free Cash Flow to Equity and Free Cash Flow to the Firm models, and Residual Income Models among others. If it involves a cash flow, it is certain that it can be discounted back to the present. The next step is to forecast the future cash flows, and the last step is to determine the ap-propriate discount rate or required rate of return that accu-rately depicts the current investment environment.

The underlying assumption regarding present value models is that there is a time value to money. If presented with two in-vestments, investment A was paying $100 today or investment B, would pay $100 in five years, which is the best choice? If the concept of time was irrelevant, most would be indifferent about which investment to choose, but if receiving $100 dollars today the option is to spend it or save it. If spending the $100, having it today rather than waiting five years to spend it makes sense, but if saved, it would earn interest. If interest rates were 10% on the $100 and it is saved it would be worth $161.05 $[100 * (1 + .10)^5]$ in five years. It does not make logi-cal sense to ever choose investment B, unless of course inves-tors were in a negative interest rate environment or deflation was underway. In a normal investment environment, inves-tors would choose investment A due to the time value of money. It would be simple to choose a discount rate if all future cash flows were known and riskless. In this case most investors would use the ten year government bond rate or a rate that more closely matches their investment horizon. Unfortu-nately, cash flows relating to stocks are never certain so there is risk involved, and when risk is involved there is a need to adjust the risk-free discount rate to reflect this risk. It is in this adjustment that causes the most trouble in proper valuation. So the basic present value calculation will build off is below.

$$V_0 = \Sigma \frac{CF_t}{(1 + r)^t}$$

V_0 = Value today
CF_t = Expected Cash flow at time t
r = The discount rate

Dividend Discount Model (DDM)

The most basic of all present value models is the dividend discount model. As the name implies this model uses dividends as the cash flow for valuation purposes. It is easy to understand why this is since the dividends are actually paid to shareholders and most companies want to maintain a stable dividend policy. Some companies do not pay dividends and theoretically can still be valued if investors can accurately anticipate when dividends will be initiated and the value of such dividends. For the purposes of this book, assume that only dividend paying companies will be analyzed using the DDM. In its most basic form, the DDM is used to value a stock based on a finite holding period return. To do this, analysts need to forecast the price the stock will sell for at the end of the investment period and all the dividends received during this period discounted back to the present. I know. How in the world can anyone do that? Please stay with me. The formula for a single period is presented here:

$$V_0 = \frac{D_1}{(1 + r)^1} + \frac{P_1}{(1 + r)^1}$$

Where:
V_0 = Value of stock today
P_1 = Expected price in one full year
D_1 = The expected dividend in the first full year
r = *discount rate/required return*

If the holding period is expected to be more than one year or one period, the equation is expanded as follows:

$$V_0 = \frac{D_1}{(1+r)^1} + \frac{D_2}{(1+r)^2} + \frac{P_2}{(1+r)^2}$$

This equation can be expanded upon for as many periods as the analyst feels comfortable forecasting, which is likely few. If it were possible to accurately forecast all dividends into the future the above equation simplifies to:

$$V_0 = \sum_{t-1}^{\infty} \frac{D_t}{(1+r)^t}$$

As the above equation shows, the need to forecast the terminal value is now irrelevant, and the ability for anyone to forecast a company's dividends into the infinite future is highly unlikely. To address this issue of forecasting, analysts often use growth rates and or growth patterns. The first of these growth pattern forecasting tools under consideration is the Gordon Growth Model (GGM)[3]. The GGM is a constant growth dividend discount model. This model was popularized by Myron J. Gordon in the late fifties and early sixties and assumes dividends will grow at a constant rate forever. This formula introduces a new component, the growth rate, g. Assuming the dividends grow at a constant rate the mathematical expres-

[3] Gordon, Myron J. (1959). "Dividends, Earnings and Stock Prices." *Review of Economics and Statistics* **41** (2): 99–105.

sion is derived by taking the current dividend, D_0, and multiplying it by one plus the growth rate to arrive at the dividend for next period.

$$D_1 = D_0(1 + g)$$

Divide D_1 by the difference between the required rate of return and the expected constant growth rate to arrive at GGM. The GGM formula is below.

$$V_0 = \frac{D_1}{r - g}$$

This is an elegant and easy to understand formula, agreed? As stated before, clarity is best gained through an example of how the GGM will value a company that pays $1.00 today is expected to grow its dividends by 10% forever and has a required rate of return of 20%. If valued today, this company it would be worth:

$$\$11.00 = \frac{1.00\,(1.10)}{.20 - .10}$$

Arriving at the growth rate is one of the most difficult tasks that an investor using this method will face. If the equation is studied or tested, it may reveal that if the required rate is less than the growth rate, the formula is invalid. This formula is not designed for companies that are in a rapid or even a high growth rate. In order for a company to qualify for this simplified equation, it needs to be growing dividends at a rate that is slower or close to the overall growth rate of the economy. This can be measured by nominal GDP. The companies that generally qualify for this type of analysis are big blue-chip companies that have a long history of steady dividend growth. The

reason a company must meet these somewhat stringent guidelines is easy to understand. If a company is growing at a rapid
pace, this cannot continue forever and as the name suggest
this formula anticipates a constant growth rate. If a company's
growth will eventually slow down, a multi-stage growth model
must be used. Often the DDM is used to value an equity index
since it encompasses the average of several companies and
generally has a stable dividend rate. A final comment is necessary regarding the denominator in the GGM equation.
When dividing the next period's dividend by the difference between the required rate and growth rate, investors are assuming this spread will continue indefinitely and thus gives us the
"constant" component of the equation. If investors did not expect the dividends to grow, this equation would transform into
the equation for a perpetuity, $V_0 = \frac{D_1}{r}$. It is evident that starting with a dividend growth rate that is equivalent to the overall growth rate of the economy when attempting to value very
large stable companies using the GGM makes sense. In the
following section is a more in depth examination at the long-
term growth rate known as the sustainable growth rate.

Multistage Dividend Discount Models

There are two popular multistage dividend discount models.
First, the two-stage DDM which assumes two distinct growth
rate phases exist for a company, and the H-Model which assumes growth rates will slowly revert to a normal stable level
over a certain time period. The previous section explained that
it is not likely that many of today's companies will grow at a
stable rate indefinitely. Many big blue-chip companies are ma-
ture and have for years had stable growth rates, for example
General Electric (GE); however, at times any company can
stimulate growth at higher levels if it branches out into a new
industry or sees rapid growth in new technologies. This inval-
idates using the Gordon DDM since growth would no longer be
stable for an indefinite period.

Two-Stage DDM

If using a dividend discount model, an investor should use a multistage model for any company that will have unsustainable growth rates. The two-stage model assumes that a company will grow at a rapid or high rate for a short period of time before suddenly changing to a sustainable growth rate. This too is unlikely for most firms, and this issue is clarified with the H-Model[4]. It is important to understand the basics for forecasting and present value calculations. The two-stage model calculation is below.

$$V_0 = \sum_{t=1}^{n} \frac{D_0(1 + g_s)^t}{(1 + r)^t} + \frac{D_0(1 + g_s)^t(1 + g_l)}{(1 + r)^t(r - g_l)}$$

$$g_l = sustainable\ growth\ rate\ or\ long-term\ growth$$
$$g_s = Short-term\ unsustainably\ high\ growth\ rate$$
$$r = required\ rate\ of\ return$$
$$D_0 = Todays\ dividend$$

Looking at this equation might lead an investor to believe that it is complicated. It is actually simple. All that is needed are the three rates of return. The long-term growth rate or sustainable growth rate can be calculated using a simple formula.

Sustainable growth rate = ROE * earnings retention rate

Look at the return on equity or ROE and multiply this by the retention rate is what is known as the sustainable growth rate. The retention rate is the percentage of earnings that are not paid out in dividends. So if a company earns $1.00 per share and has a retention rate of 40%, the company retains $0.40 per

---

[4] The H-Model was developed by Fuller and Hsia (1984)

share and pays out $0.60 per share as dividends to its share-
holders. As with all financial theory, there is a judgment call
to be made for all growth rates. In order for the sustainable
growth rate to hold true for the long-term rate, investors must
assumed that the ROE is sustainable and that the company
plans to maintain its current dividend policy. If a company
under analysis pays a $1.00 dividend and is growing at an un-
sustainable growth rate of 30% per year, and it is thought this
will continue for three years and drop to a long-term sustainable growth rate of 10%. If an investor requires a 15% rate of
return, they can utilize the data in the above formula to arrive
at a value for the company. Assume the market price is $30.00.
The value based on the above two-stage dividend discount
model is as follows:

$$V_0 = \frac{1(1.30)^3}{(1.15)^3} + \frac{1(1.30)^3(1.10)}{(1.15)^3(.15-.10)} = \$33.25$$

Based on the data and the assumed growth rates from above,
it appears this company is undervalued. If the analysis is correct, an investor could buy the stock today for $30.00 and an-
ticipate that the intrinsic value is worth at least $33.25. That
is a 10% return if the analysis proves correct. The most important fact to remember about this type of model is that the
right-hand side of the equation is where the majority of the
value is derived. This is called the terminal value of the stock
which is the value of the stock based on the sustainable growth
rate thought to continue forever. In the above equation $31.80
is the present value of the terminal value and only $1.45 con-
tributes to the present value of the stock based on the present
value of dividends. This informs an investor that any error in
forecasting of growth or required rates can cause huge devia-
tions in the forecast of value. This is the largest drawback for
this model and some analysts will use growth rate bands to
forecast a range of terminal values. This will give them an

idea of the relative value compared to where the stock is currently trading.

The H-Model

As was mentioned before, it is unlikely that a company grows
rapidly and suddenly slows to a sustainable growth rate in-
stantaneously. The H-model addresses this issue. The H-
model offers a smooth transition to the sustainable growth rate
that declines linearly.

$$V_0 = \frac{D_0(1 + g_l) + D_0H(g_s - g_l)}{(r - g_l)}$$

The only new term in this equation is the "H" which stands for
the half-life of the rapid growth period. So if investors expect
the rapid growth of a company to last 10 years, they would plug
in 5 in place of the H, this represents half of the 10-year rapid
growth rate. The left side of the numerator is similar to the
Gordon Growth Model as it assumes the sustainable growth
rate will go on indefinitely. The right side of the equation
shows the difference between the rapid and long-term growth
rate almost like an accrual account for the difference that the
extra return provides in terms of dividend growth. To simplify
this equation, the right side of the equation is "extra value"
that is due to the extra return from the abnormally high
growth period. Like most other financial models the more inputs that are estimated, the more error prone the model is, especially for a new investor. The drawbacks to this style of
valuation is that it is assumed that growth rates will be constant or that growth rates will follow a smooth transition to a
more stable growth rate which is often not the case. The largest drawback to the present value discount models is that
nearly all the value of a stock is derived from a stock's terminal
value. This cannot be stressed enough. As discussed, the terminal value is extremely sensitive to miscalculations of growth

rates and can be disastrous if under or overvalued by only a small fraction. Even with the drawbacks, it is important to understand and to implement present value discount models as part of an overall investment toolkit. When using dividends as the cash flows in the present value model, it is important to understand when to apply this type of model and when it is best to apply a different model. For the DDM, a company needs to, of course, pay a dividend as well as have a stable dividend policy. A stable dividend policy is one that does not fluctuate erratically and is aligned with the profitability of the company. Generally this model is most reliable with well-established companies that are not a part of the fast growing industries more susceptible to wide swings in earnings and dividends.

Cash Flow Models (FCFE & FCFF)

The previous section used a company's dividends as the basis for cash flows and future cash flows. This section uses free cash flow to value a company. Dividends are actually paid to shareholders and are fairly easy to forecast when a company has a stable dividend policy. Free cash flows on the other hand are not readily available, and investors will need to calculate these quantities from financial reports such as the income statement. Free cash flows are not actually paid out to the investor but are available to be paid out.

For the purpose of valuation, free cash flows are generally divided into two distinct groups, Free Cash Flow to Equity (FCFE) and Free Cash Flow to the Firm (FCFF). FCFE can be used to value the equity of a company directly whereas FCFF values the company as a whole. FCFF can also be used to value the equity of a company after it has been adjusted for debt. In the previous section the cash flows (dividends) were directly measured and easy to determine. This section will spend more time on the process of determining the cash flows used in the valuation.

First, define these cash flows. FCFF is the cash flow from operations minus capital expenditures or capex for short. FCFF is the cash flow available to all suppliers of capital, which would include both debt and equity, after all operating expenses (including taxes) have been paid and the firm has made its investments in working capital and fixed capital. Do not be confused by other cash flow measures such as cash flow from operations (CFO) as these cash flows are not accurate for use in a discounted cash flow (DCF) model. However, FCFE and FCFF can be calculated from CFO as well as from other financial statement metrics.

There are several ways to arrive at FCFE and FCFF from other sources found within financial statements. First, here are two ways of calculated FCFE and FCFF. The most common forms of calculating FCFF and FCFE are from net income and cash flow from operations. By looking at how to calculate FCFF and FCFE it is possible to move on the present value models.

Arriving at FCFF

When talking about FCFF, remember that this is only the cash that *could* be distributed to all suppliers of capital. If a business owner has cash coming in the door from customers, what is the priority of where to use this cash: pay bills and buy or build more inventory, right? All the things that keep the doors open. This is the working capital. If it is necessary to purchase additional equipment or build another facility, this the investment in fixed capital, which goes beyond keeping the business open like the working capital component but allows for expansion of operations. Once a company pays its bills and invests cash back into the company to continue to grow, hopefully the business has cash left over for its owners. This is the cash flow investors are interested in since this is the cash flow that theoretically belongs to owners or creditors. To arrive at FCFF from net income, combine the working capital and fixed capital investments and add to net income (NI) non-cash charges. There are several things that are considered non-cash charges such as restructuring charges and gains and losses, but the most common non-cash charge is depreciation and amortization. Depreciation and amortization will be the focus for this book. After-tax interest expense is subtracted to arrive at NI, this too needs to be added back to NI. So the calculation for FCFF starting with a net income figure is:

$$FCFF = NI + NC + INT(1\text{-}T) - INV\ FA - INV\ WC$$

Where:
NI = Net income
NC = Non-cash Charges (Depreciation/Amortization)
INT(1-T) = After-tax Interest
INV FA = Investment in Fixed Assets
INV WC = Investment in Working Capital

The next method used for computing FCFF is starting with CFO. The next topic will discuss how to arrive at each of the inputs and where to locate them with the financial statements.

$$FCFF = CFO + INT(1\text{-}T) - INV\ FA$$

The above equations are the most common forms in determining the value of FCFF. Going forward it is necessary to assume that an investor has a moderate understanding of financial statement analysis. If not, studying this subject is a prerequisite but not a requirement to understanding this part of the book which will review the basics of course but will not go deep into the determinants of the inputs required as this is beyond the scope of this book. Looking at the inputs and where they are found in the financial statements is the next step.

Net income is the easiest to find and of course is located in the income statement. It is the bottom line so to speak of a company's earnings after subtracting all expenses including interest and taxes but before dividends are paid to common shareholders. Assume for the purpose of simplicity that depreciation and amortization are the only non-cash charges since they are the most common. Depreciation expense is located in the income statement as well. The after-tax interest expense is also added back to net income because interest expenses reduce the overall tax bill paid by a company and therefore it is necessary to add to net income the interest multiplied by one minus the tax rate. Interest expense is also located in the income statement.

Next locate and subtract from net income the investment in fixed assets. Capital expenditures for fixed assets are located in the balance sheet and investors must remember to calculate the increase from the prior period and not the total amount. So if fixed assets were $100 in 2013 and $150 in 2014, the investment in fixed assets is not the total amount from the balance sheet of $150 but the difference between the two amounts, $50.

Investment in working capital is also derived from the balance sheet and the cash flow statement. Since the objective is to calculate the free cash flow available for distribution which is the change in cash from the prior period, subtract cash from current assets to get a truer picture of the free cash flows. So in order to find the increase or decrease in working capital, take current assets minus the cash portion and subtract the current liabilities from this total. This is similar to the calculation for fixed asset investments when looking for the increase or decrease from the prior period to plug into the FCFF formula and not the total amount for a given year. This is crucial to remember and is a common mistake made by beginner investors attempting to utilize FCFF company valuations.

Let us look at how to arrive at FCFF starting with cash from operations (CFO). Start with CFO located in the statement of cash flows, this eliminates a few inputs from the formula used starting with net income since CFO has already incorporated them. For example do not add back non-cash charges since CFO has already incorporated the needed adjustments. Another input to ignore in the CFO calculation is the working capital investment as the CFO has already made the adjustments for this as well. To utilize this equation, pull the CFO from the statement of cash flows, add the after-tax interest expense just like in the net income equation,   and subtract the investment in fixed assets.

With the basics for FCFF calculations in hand, the next step is to address FCFE. FCFE are the free cash flows that are available to both equity providers as well as credit providers. FCFE on the other hand are the free cash flows that are available to the equity providers to the company. It is a less burdensome to calculate the value of a stock using the FCFE cash flow as opposed to the FCFF. Basically once the calculation for FCFF has been accomplished, make a few common sense adjustments in order to arrive at FCFE. Remember to subtract the other providers of capital from the equations. The formula is below:

$$FCFE = FCFF - Int(1\text{-}T) + \text{Additional Borrowing}$$

As demonstrated in the above equations, FCFE is the cash flow that is available to its shareholders. This is a simple adjustment that allows investors to focus on the cash flows that are important to them.

Now that the method for determining FCFE and FCFF has been clarified, the next step is valuation. FCFE and FCFF models use the same logic as other discounted cash flow models. The only difference between the free cash flow valuation models and the dividend valuation models is the cash flow being used. The main difference between FCFE and FCFF models is the discount rate or required return used in discounting the cash flow back to the present. A new term called the weighted average cost of capital (WACC) is now necessary. This incorporates the after-tax cost of debt into the required rate of return. Use the WACC to discount back the FCFF to the present. Recall from the section on the CAPM that the formula for CAPM was used to determine the cost of equity, which is the return used to discount back FCFE. To calculate the WACC utilize the capital structure of the company as well as its tax rate and cost of debt. The capital structure is determined by how much of a company is financed by debt and how much is equity. If a company is 40% financed by debt and 60% financed by equity the WACC consists of using the weight of debt which is 40% multiplied by the after-tax cost of debt and the weight of equity, 60%, multiplied by the cost of equity. To arrive at a company's capital structure use the following equation:

The percentage of a company financed by debt =
Market value of Debt / (Market value of Debt + Market value of Equity)

The percentage of a company financed by equity =
Market value of Equity / (Market value of Debt + Market value of Equity)

The formula for WACC is below:

$$WACC = \%D(rd)(1\text{-}T) + \%E(re)$$

Where:
%D = Percentage of a company finance by debt
rd = Cost of debt
T = Corporate tax rate
%E = Percentage of a company finance by equity
re = Cost of equity

Since the FCFF is the total free cash flows for all suppliers of capital, it is fitting to use a discount rate that incorporates both the cost of debt and cost of equity, which is the WACC. The FCFE uses the required rate of return for equity to discount back its cash flows. When FCFF is discounted back to the present, there is a clear value for the entire firm, not just the equity. In order to obtain the value of equity from the value of the entire firm, subtract the market value of debt. The present value of FCFF is calculated as follows:

$$\textbf{Value of entire firm} = \sum_{t=1}^{\infty} \frac{FCFF_t}{(1+WACC)^t}$$

The same calculation is used for FCFE but substitute the WACC with the required rate of return, r.

$$\textbf{Value of equity} = \sum_{t=1}^{\infty} \frac{FCFE_t}{(1+r)^t}$$

The equation for a constant growth rate assumption is the same as that of the dividend models except for the discount rate for the FCFF. Consider this review.

$$\textbf{Value of entire firm} = \sum_{t=1}^{\infty} \frac{FCFF_0(1+g)}{WACC-g}$$

$$\textbf{Value of equity} = \sum_{t=1}^{\infty} \frac{FCFE_0(1+g)}{r-g}$$

As is clear, there is no difference in the former DDM and the new free cash flow model equations because both use the same concept for discounting to the present all future cash flows as is true for all present value models.

The two-stage models for FCFE and FCFF are below.

$$\text{Value of the Firm} = \sum_{t=1}^{n} \frac{FCFF_t}{(1+WACC)^t} + \frac{FCFF_{n+1}}{(WACC-g)}\left(\frac{1}{(1+WACC)^n}\right)$$

$$\text{Value of the Equity of the Firm} = \sum_{t=1}^{n} \frac{FCFE_t}{(1+r)^t} + \frac{FCFE_{n+1}}{(r-g)}\left(\frac{1}{(1+g)^n}\right)$$

As demonstrated in the above equation, the two-stage FCFF is the sum of the present value of future cash flows growing at the extraordinary growth period and the present value of the terminal price at the end of the period. Investors or analysts can use any of the present value equations by plugging in FCFF or FCFE where the dividend, D, is present. One major difference in the dividend models and the free cash flow models is that free cash flow growth is often determined by modeling sales and profitability as opposed to forecasting the free cash flows directly, although some analysts choose to do this. As with the DDMs from the previous sections, one main drawback to using this model is that the terminal value makes up the majority of the present value of a stock. Investors may be thinking the above equation looks nothing like the DDM. It is because of this difference in growth rates, that investors use the $FCFF_t$ instead of $FCFF(1 + g)^t$ although it is perfectly fine to do so. The majority of the time FCFF or FCFE are forecast for each individual period instead of using the constant growth rates.

One thing to mention before moving on is that when calculating the FCFF value there are a few adjustments that need to be made if the goal is to value the company's stock. First, make the adjustments mentioned above to arrive at the value of equity. After determining the value of equity, divide this number by the number of shares outstanding to find the value of equity per share.

FCFE and FCFF valuation models are best used when a company does not pay dividends or the dividend policy is not stable or if the investor is looking at valuing the company from a control perspective. When using the DDM models, investors are at the mercy of the board of directors in terms of receiving cash flow in terms of dividends, in essence investors have no control. However if considering the purchase of the entire company, investors will control the dividend distributions and therefore control the distributions to shareholders.

The next logical question is how to forecast FCFF and FCFE. Some analysts attempt to forecast free cash flows directly or use a constant growth rate. Forecasting FCFF and FCFE can be quite overwhelming for the beginner as most analysts build complex pro-forma financial statements.

This book is an attempt to take somewhat complex information and condense it in to bite size pieces. The reference page of this book should be enough to provide investors with advanced knowledge of any of the topics within this book. So keeping with this theme, this book will not attempt to explain the more complex issues and advanced techniques of pro forma financial statement analysis and will use the constant growth rate assumption. The point is to grasp the concept and have the knowledge to implement this within a portfolio if an individual investor or within a client's accounts if an investment advisor.

This chapter has been rather labor intensive but is necessary in order to grasp the valuation process. Here is an example that will clarify the free cash flow valuation models.

Let us evaluate McDonalds (MCD) beginning in 2013. Estimated inputs for MCD's for our valuation model are as follows:

FCFE: $5.271.4 Billion.
Risk-free rate: 1.80%
Beta: 0.80
The equity risk premium: 8.0%

The first thing to do is to calculate the required rate of return for MCD. Do this using the CAPM as follows:

$.065 = .018 + .8*(.08)$

The required rate of return is 6.5% for MCD and the growth rate of FCFF over the last three years is 0.96%. To find the present value of equity, use the FCFE equation:

$$\frac{5271.4 * (1.0096)}{(0.065 - .0096)} = 96,064.98$$

The value of MCD's equity is $96,064.98 million dollars. Stock investors do not want to value the equity of the company because they are interested in buying on a per share basis. So make one final adjust and that is to divide the total equity value by the number of shares outstanding. MCD has 990.4 million shares outstanding. So MCD is worth:

$$\frac{96,064.98}{990.4} = \$96.996 \ or \ \$97.00$$

This evaluation is accomplished by making a few key assumptions. The first was that the growth rate of FCFE would continue to grow at the three year average forever, which was a little less than one percent. Another assumption was that CAPM was used to calculate the required rate of return. These assumptions can cause wild valuations. For example, suppose the estimated required rate of return was 15%. This would have dropped the assumed intrinsic value to below $40 per share. Once again this reinforces the importance of proper rate analysis.

Residual Income Model

Another popular present value model that has gained momentum is the Residual Income model. As the name implies, residual income is the income in excess of the required income that shareholders demand for investing capital. This may be best illustrated with an example. If all equity shareholders contribute $1,000,000 as an investment in a company, using the CAPM, the required return is 10% for all shareholders. Suppose the company earns $50,000 over the next year. Has this company actually added any value to its shareholders? The company has made a positive net profit but failed to make a profit efficient enough to cover the opportunity cost of the equity shareholders. The required return that shareholders demand is $100,000 ($1,000,000 * 10%); however, the company only earned $50,000. The residual income is actually negative which means the company is destroying value. Now suppose the company earned $500,000. Now the residual income or economic value is $400,000 ($500,000 - $100,000). This is the value above the shareholders' required return the company has provided to its shareholders.

The residual income model again uses the same present value equations as before though the cash flow being measured and forecast is residual income. What separates residual income from other earnings metrics is that it takes into account the additional cost of equity capital, not just debt capital. The income statement is a statement to the owners of the company that shows the accounting profitability of the firm. It takes into consideration the cost of debt in the form of interest paid over the reporting period; however, there is not a charge or cost of equity against net income. Looking at the above example clarifies that the required rate of return on equity is used to show the expense of using equity capital which is subtracted from earnings to arrive at residual income. A novice investor may not be familiar with the term residual income but may recognize its other aliases such as economic profit or economic value added all of which measure residual income. Here is a view of the Residual Income model formula.

$$Value\ today = B_0 + \sum_{t=1}^{\infty} \frac{E_t - rB_{t-1}}{(1+r)^t}$$

Where:
B_0 = Today's book value per share
B_t = Expected book value per share at time t
r = Required rate of return
E_t = Expected Earnings per share at time t
$E_t - rB_{t-1}$ = Residual Income

The above equation states that the intrinsic value of a stock today is equal to its current book value (Book value is sometimes referred to as equity) plus the sum of all future residual income discounted back to the present by the required rate of return. The numerator states that residual income is equal to earnings in the period being analyzed minus the equity charge which is the required rate of return multiplied by last period's book value or ending book value.

If residual income is expected to grow at a constant rate, modify the above equation to:

$$V_0 = B_0 + \frac{ROE - r}{r - g} B_0$$

How is this equation an evolution from the above equation since they do not resemble each other at all? There is a logical reason. If a company's ROE is greater than its required rate of return, the company will have a positive residual income. If a company's ROE is less than its required rate of return, it will

have a negative residual income. As earlier stated, equity multiplied by the required rate of return is the hurdle rate for net
income that a company must make in order to have positive
residual income. Since ROE is the sum of net income divided
by equity, it is logical that if ROE is greater than the required
rate, r, residual income must be positive. Looking back at the
previous example, if net income is $500,000 and equity is val-
ued at $1,000,000, ROE is 50%. Since the required rate of re-
turn on equity was only 10%, there is a residual income of
$400,000 [(.5 - .1) * 1,000,000 = $400,000] which is the same
answer as above.

Recall the discussion on growth rates using the DDM under
the assumption of multiple growth rates, in a constant growth
rate environment investors can obtain the growth rate using
the retention rate and ROE. A company's retention rate is the
amount of earnings a company retains versus the amount it
pays out as dividends or uses to buy back shares. If ROE remains constant, multiply it by the retention rate to obtain
what is called the sustainable growth rate. Consider a simple
example. Suppose a company has the following characteristics:

The required rate of return: 10%
ROE: 15%
Retention rate: 50%
Book value of equity per share today: $10

What is the intrinsic value of this stock based on the constant
growth rate residual income model?

$$V_0 = 10 + \frac{(.15-.1)}{(.1-.075)} * 10 = \$30$$

This hypothetical company is worth $30 per share based on the
residual income model. If the market price is below this value

today, the stock is undervalued, and the stock is overvalued if the market price today is more than this value. A quick way to check whether a company is creating or destroying value is to compile a simple ratio. Take the return on invested capital (ROIC) which is, $\frac{Net\ Income - Dividends}{Total\ Capital}$, and divide it by the WACC. If the value is greater than one, the company is creating wealth for its shareholders. This is plainly a different way of stating that a company is generating positive residual income. The return being generated is higher than the cost to generate it.

As with other models, it is possible to use the residual income model to forecast residual income over a finite investment period. There are some differences to address. It is assumed that a company cannot maintain a stable and steady ROE forever and that competition either boosts ROE or diminishes it. ROE typically reverts to the cost of equity over time. This happens mainly because of competitive forces. A company with a high ROE will draw the attention of competitors. As new companies enter the market, ROE begins to diminish and moves towards its required rate of return. This also causes residual income to decrease overtime, and if ROE equals the required rate of return, residual income falls to zero. Another difference is the fact that the terminal value using the residual income model will not make up a large portion of the overall present value. As demonstrated in the above equations, the book value generates the majority of the intrinsic value of a company whereas in our other models the terminal value made up the majority of the value.

The last residual income model under discussion is the multistage residual income model. The focus of the multistage model is what is referred to as continuing residual income which is the residual income expected after the time horizon under analysis. As addressed in the previous paragraph, most analysts assume residual income decreases over time. Some models assume residual income falls to zero in the terminal year while some assume it falls to a positive level and maintains that positive level indefinitely. There are a wide range of models available and those are beyond the scope of this book. However, there are two worth mentioning here. The first is based on an assumption that at the end of a finite time horizon, a company will trade at a premium to book value. The equation is the same as above except for the addition of a present value calculation of the premium that is expected at the end of an investment time horizon. The P_T in the equation below is the expected price the stock is to trade at time T. The equation is below:

$$V_0 = B_0 + \sum_{t=1}^{T} \frac{E_t - r\,B_{t-1}}{(1+r)^t} + \frac{P_T - B_T}{(1+r)^T}$$

Or

$$V_0 = B_0 + \sum_{t=1}^{T} \frac{(ROE - r)\,B_{t-1}}{(1+r)^t} + \frac{P_T - B_T}{(1+r)^T}$$

Most literature on the subject states that if the forecast period is long, the book value premium should be close to zero, but if the forecast period is short, say two years, then a relevant premium is required.

The last equation attempts to quantify that residual income and ROE tend to fade over time. Dechow, Hutton, and Sloan (1998) created a residual income model with what they call a persistence factor. The persistence factor is between zero and one, with a value of one meaning the residual income will not fade over time and will remain constant. The higher the persistence factor the higher the terminal residual income which in turn means a higher intrinsic value.

$$V_0 = B_0 + \sum_{t=1}^{T-1} \frac{E_t - rB_{T-1}}{(1+r)^t} + \frac{E_t - rB_{T-1}}{(1+r-\omega)(1+r)^{T-1}}$$

The ω in the above equation is the persistence factor that will converge the residual income toward zero over time. This is likely the most practical residual income model, yet determining the persistence factor for a company can be quite tedious.

The residual income model seems fairly simple since investors do not need to forecast earnings and the terminal value does not make up a majority of a company's intrinsic value. The problem with the residual income model is that investors must assume that clean surplus accounting holds true all the time. Clean surplus means that all gains and losses go through the income statement and that the ending book value or equity is equal to current book plus earnings minus dividends. This is not true in every situation since companies at times have other comprehensive income that bypass the income statement as well as accounting items such as unrealized gains and losses on securities held for sale. There are many more items that can skew the assumed clean surplus accounting outputs assumed to hold true under the residual income model. This does not mean the model is irrelevant; it means a better understanding of the accounting of corporate profits is needed to fully utilize the residual income model. An analyst will need to have an understanding of the company under analysis' accounting policies.

Valuation equations may seem tedious and boring, but it is important to have an understanding of how some analysts value a company using present value models. The above equations are the building blocks for many investors who go on to develop their own ways of valuing a company. Again, there is not a scientifically right or wrong way to value a company. Some analysts are skilled enough to use multiple models depending on the circumstances of the company. Multiple assumptions and forecasts often leave would-be investors with too much uncertainty. So as promised I will share one way that I developed to value stocks. There is nothing scientific or Nobel worthy in this valuation model; it is my assumptions and expectations regarding companies that I tend to favor when investing. It does not take a genius to develop and implement a successful investment strategy. It requires a never give up attitude and thirst for knowledge that is unquenchable. I have given up on trying to develop a fail prove investment strategy. Instead I believe it is better to be consistent than perfect when it comes to investing because it is impossible to be perfect in the financial world.

vStat Valuation

The vStat valuation model is a present value model that does not attempt to use a theoretical model for growth rate determination or for a required rate of return. It is my common sense model and is based solely on my own expectations and assumptions as the most desirable price to pay for a company. It is not specific in any way. If the vStat valuation model gives an intrinsic value for a stock, it does not represent where the price of a stock should be. It gives an idea as to whether or not an investor is paying too much for a company based on subjective expectations.

The first task is to determine the growth rate for the company being analyzed. To do this, take the growth estimates based on other analysts' expectations for the 3-5 year growth rate. I use Bloomberg's long-term growth rate for this number. To adjust for the error in expectations, project a median value for ROE over the last eight quarters and multiply this by the average retention ratio over the same eight quarter period. Recognizing the ROE multiplied by the retention ratio is the sustainable growth rate mentioned earlier. However, to smooth the data to get a more accurate picture of a sustainable growth rate, take the median value of ROE and attempt to eliminate any extreme outliers where ROE is unusually high or low which will cause the growth rate to be skewed to either the upside or the downside. From two sets of estimated growth rates, take the average.

g = (Analyst Estimate of 3-5yr Growth Rate + Median ROE over eight quarters * Average Retention Rate over Eight Quarters)/2

Next project earnings per share over the next three years. Do not assume any longer than that because growth rates could be inaccurate, and the further out the attempted forecast, the larger an error will be. Remember also that an active investor will make the necessary adjustments each time the companies report updated financial statements. This helps recognize forecasting errors and offers the opportunity to cut losses before they grow too large. To forecast the future value of earnings per share, use the trailing twelve month (TTM) earnings per share (EPS) number and plug it in to the future value equation using my assumed growth rate.

$$Estimated\ EPS\ in\ 3yrs = EPS_{3yr} = EPS_{ttm} * (1 + g)^3$$

Now an investor needs to know the value of this company in three years. To accomplish this it is important to know what multiple based on the Price to earnings multiple (P/E) this company "should" trade for three years from now. This of course is a huge assumption, so take a conservative approach by taking the lower of either the current P/E or two times the growth rate (g). So if a company has a P/E today of 10 and the growth rate is 10%, use the P/E today with a value of 10 as opposed to the absolute value of 20 (2*10) based on twice the growth rate. This is a crude way of estimating the value of a company three years from today, but the goal is not to get a true intrinsic value. It is an attempt to value a company based on as conservative an estimate as feasible. Multiply the P/E by EPS_{3yr} to arrive at the price this company could sell for three years from today.

$$\text{Price of stock in 3yrs} = P_{3yr} = Est.\frac{P}{E} * EPS_{3yr}$$

As learned earlier, in order to get the present value of a stock today based on the price estimate in the future, there needs to be a required rate of return. Financial theory provides a beautiful equation to determine the required rate of return called the CAPM, and it is great in theory, but in practical real life valuation, it does not hold up. Do not be afraid to explore individual requirements for rates of return, but I prefer to discount the price of a stock by 15%.

$$P_0 = \frac{EPS_{3yr}}{(1+.15)^3}$$

This is my required rate of return. It is what I demand from a company in order to invest money. The number could be and likely is different. The larger the required rate of return used in a present value calculation, the smaller the present value will be. So if the required rate of return is 25%, the price an investor is willing to pay for the same company will be lower than mine. There are outliers when utilizing such crude methods for valuation, but over time an investor will recognize that when intrinsic value is four times the current price of a stock, growth rate assumptions were out of line. This is not a valuation process to follow blindly and is only one of many that I use to determine if a stock's price today is going to be a good investment in the future or whether I should pass.

Let us theoretically analyze a hypothetical company, ABC with the following characteristics:

Earnings Per share TTM: $1.00
Current P/E : 10
Analyst's Estimates 3-5 Year Growth Rate: 5%
Median ROE over 8 Quarters: 25%
Average Retention Rate over 8 Quarters: 25%

In order to get a valuation for this company, work through the following steps:

1. Determine a growth rate by taking the median ROE of 25% and multiplying it by the retention rate. .25 * .25 = .0625 or 6.25%

2. The 3-5 Year Growth rate based on analyst expectations is 5%. To obtain growth rate, average steps 1 and 2. This would give a growth rate of 5.625%.

3. To arrive at an expected P/E ratio, use the lower between current P/E of 10 and two times the growth rate. Two times the growth rate of 5.625% is 11.25. So use the current P/E of 10.

4. Determine the EPS of ABC three years from now and accomplish this by taking the current EPS of $1.00 and calculating the future value.

$$1 * (1.0625)^3 = \$1.199 = EPS_{3\,yr}$$

5. If EPS in three years will be $1.119 and there is a current P/E of 10, the price ABC could be trading for $11.99 in three years.

6. To know what investors will pay for ABC today if the required rate of return was 15%. This would be $\frac{11.99}{1.15^3} =$ $7.89.

This asserts that if ABC is trading for less than $7.89 it would be on sale based on this valuation methodology.

[6]

Relative Valuation

The last chapter was a little intense for most beginner investors trying to grasp the fundamentals of valuation. I would recommend rereading it to keep the ideas fresh. Relative valuation is the valuation most financial advisors use to communicate with clients and most analysts use in stock reports because relative valuation uses price or enterprise value multiples to value a stock or to compare one stock to another. For the investor unfamiliar with this term, price multiples are ratios of a company's stock price to a fundamental factor, such as earnings, while enterprise value multiples take into consideration all capital providers and therefore are used to value the entire company. The use of price multiples is wide spread due to the simplicity of the calculation. With most price multiples there is no need to forecast fundamental values or discount back to the present some estimated figure. Investors often think price multiples are the complete opposite of present value models, but this could not be further from the truth. One thing to keep in mind is that the price multiple of an asset should be related to the expected future cash flows. An investor can relate the price of a stock to any fundamental factor to determine whether it is expensive or cheap when compared to other companies within the same industry, a benchmark multiple, or to itself. The main goal of relative valuation is to determine whether a company is over-valued, undervalued, or fairly valued when compared against peers or even the company's own prior history.

There are two main methods for using multiples. One is known as the method of comparables. This method takes the approach of valuing a company based on some price or enter-prise multiple for the company under analysis compared to a company with similar assets or in the same industry or a group of similar companies. The other method of relative valuation is the forecasted fundamentals method. This method uses forecasted fundamentals and can be used with present value models to determine the value of a company. I will not attempt to cover each variable in detail but will give a broad overview in hopes of providing a good foundation for multiple valuation.

Method of Comparables Using the P/E

The underlying philosophy behind the method of comparables is similar assets should sell for similar prices. This is some-times easier said than done. Let us begin the study with the most common price multiple the P/E ratio. Why would an an-alyst want to examine the P/E ratio? The P/E tells an investor how much is being paid for the earnings of a company.

To calculate the P/E ratio, determine the market price and the earnings for the company being analyzed. Verify that the de-nominator uses the same time frame and measurement before comparing two different company P/E's. The comparison could be drastically skewed if using the last fiscal year of earnings for one company and the average of four quarters of earnings for another company. If the same data vendor is used for both companies, the information should be fine. There are many alternative ways for calculating the P/E ratio. Some use the trailing twelve month EPS figures which is known as the trailing P/E, while others use the forward P/E which uses next year's estimated EPS in the calculation. Other variations include using diluted EPS or basic EPS for the denominator. The only certainty about calculating the P/E is the current market price.

If an investor was thinking about investing in a gumball manufacturer that is currently priced in the market at $50 per share and had $5 of earnings per share, the P/E can be calculated by taking the price divided by the earnings which would be 10. This number informs the investor that for every dollar of earnings that this company generates per share, an investor would pay $10. The financial community would say the investor is "paying ten times earnings." To those new to investing, paying ten times earnings sounds ridiculous, but a seasoned investor knows a P/E of ten is not ridiculous. The P/E ratio when used to compare one company to similar companies or to an industry as a whole can be misleading. I see many investors fail to utilize the P/E ratio correctly because they misinterpret the underlying fundamentals. Financial advisors have all heard someone say, "This company is a buy because it is trading at a low P/E." The reality is an investor must still know the underlying fundamental drivers of a company's earnings in order to make sound financial decisions when using price multiples. Revisit the gumball manufacturer and compare it to one of its competitors that is currently trading at a P/E of 20. Is this company too expensive or a worse investment than our gumball manufacturer with a P/E of 10? The beginner investor may determine that the P/E of 10 is more attractive and base a purchasing decision on the fact that the gumball manufacturer has a lower P/E. Now what if the gumball manufacturer was growing its earnings at 5% per year and the competitor was growing their earnings at 50% per year. Would this change an investor's mind? Keep in mind that in order to use the method of comparables, find an actual comparable company. Do not assume that since two companies are in the same industry that they are comparable to each other. Make sure the capital structure as well as the assets of each firm are comparable, among other things. Comparing apples to oranges can really land an investor in a world of confusion.

Analysts often find differences within the fundamentals of the company and the peer company or peer group under analysis. This is likely the reason for analyzing the company in the first place. When using the P/E to compare valuations, keep in mind that the objective is to identify the company that has the highest expected growth rate with the least amount of risk and at the same time trading at a lower P/E multiple than its peers. This may sound simple, but in practice it can be quite painful when trying to determine a company's true risk and growth rate while at the same time making sure both are comparable.

There will be times when earnings for a company are negative and cause the investor to wonder if the P/E ratio can be negative. Mathematically it is possible, but realistically it is meaningless in stock valuation. To use the price and earnings to compare a company to its peers when the company under analysis has negative earnings, use what is known as the earnings yield. The earnings yield is the reciprocal of the P/E, or E/P. Dividing the earnings by the price creates a yield. Looking back to the gumball manufacturer the market price was $50 and the EPS were $5. By dividing the EPS of $5 by the price per share of $50, we get an E/P of 10%. Since we are looking for the lowest P/E when comparing companies, a negative P/E would appear to be a better value, however in reality the negative P/E would be the most expensive. So the E/P solves this issue since investors are no longer looking for the lowest value but the highest.

There is one other thing to consider before moving on to new information. As discussed previously, discounted cash flow models require a calculation of a terminal value in order to find the intrinsic value of a stock, and this terminal value made up a majority of the intrinsic value. An investor can use price multiples to estimate the terminal value of a stock as opposed to the growth rate and required rate of return as with the Gordon growth model. The most common way to do this is by using comparable price multiples which can be based on industry data or the company's own historical data. If a candy bar company has EPS of $1.00 today and is expected to grow its earnings by 10% for the next five years, calculate the expected EPS in year five as $1.61. Assume a calculated median value for the company's peers is 10. The terminal value in year five for the candy bar company would be $16.11. This eliminates a few problems that the original DDM terminal value posed when it came to growth rates and required rates of return. As discussed in the section on discounted cash flow models, the terminal value is sensitive to even seemingly minute errors in forecasted growth rates. The market multiple method eliminates this problem but poses one of its own. If the peer group being used to arrive at the price multiple is itself over or undervalued, this causes estimates of terminal value to be over or under valued as well.

Method of Forecasting Fundamentals Using the P/E

Under the relative valuation model, an investor can use variables to compare companies to peers or benchmarks. Investors can do the same thing with the method of forecasting fundamentals and investors can also use the company's market data and compare it with it is own forecasted data. This is similar to forecasting a stock price with the exception that the investor is now attempting to use fundamental data to explain other fundamental data regarding price or valuation.

After looking closely at the Gordon Growth model, investors can directly relate the forecast derived from the model to arrive at the P/E. Since this model uses dividends as the cash flow, the next period's dividend divided by the difference between the required rate of return, r, and the expected growth rate, g, is equal to the present value of the stock today. It is possible to determine the P/E by taking the payout ratio multiplied by one plus the growth rate and divide by the difference between the required rate and growth rate.[5]

$$\frac{P_0}{E_0} = \frac{(payout\ ratio)(1+g)}{(r-g)}$$

Where:
Payout ratio $= \frac{D_0(1+g)}{E_0}$
D_0 = Dividend just paid

By using a present value model that assumes dividends will continue forever at a constant rate and discounting them back to the present, the P/E that is calculated from this equations is called the justified P/E. If the current P/E today when compared to the justified P/E is higher (lower), assume the stock is overvalued (undervalued).

An example will help clarify the above analysis. If the gumball manufacturing plant has a forecasted long-term sustainable growth rate of 10% and a long-term retention rate of 25% and the calculated required rate of return is 15%. Is the gumball company overvalued, undervalued or fairly valued? Assume the current P/E ratio is 10. The above formula would find that the justified P/E is 16.5. Since the justified P/E is greater than the current market P/E, we would conclude that the gumball manufacturer is indeed undervalued.

---

[5] All notation derived from the text Pinto et al (2010).

Method of Forecasting Fundamentals Using the Price to Book Value

It is important to briefly touch on the Price to Book value per share or P/B ratio and explain a simple valuation tool that I use to create a quick snap shot of a stock's intrinsic value. A company's book value is derived from its balance sheet and is a company's assets minus its liabilities minus any preferred shareholder dividends. One benefit to using the P/B versus the P/E is that a company's equity is generally more stable than a company's earnings. Also if a company has negative earnings, it probably will still have a positive book value per share. It is not without its own faults such as measurability of assets for comparison between peer companies. If considering the differences between book value and market value, there can be significant discrepancies. The P/B ratio measures the price per share against the equity of the company. The larger the P/B ratio the more an investor will pay for each dollar of equity. The justified P/B ratio is:

$$\frac{P_0}{B_0} = \frac{ROE - g}{r - g}$$

For example, if a hypothetical company has a return on equity (ROE) of 20%, a required rate of return of 10%, and an expected growth rate of 5%, it would have a justified P/B ratio of 3.00, ($\frac{20-5}{10-5}$). If today the company's P/B ratio is 5.00, this company is overvalued or expensive. The method of comparables for P/B is identical to the method of comparables for the P/E as previously discussed.

A very simple forecasting method using Book value per share, P/E, and ROE is possible. I will use data gathered from the financial statements for McDonalds (MCD) to project out the next quarter's forecasted price. This is simple and should not be confused with true fundamental valuation. However, when in a pinch for time to make an analysis, I forecast the next period's price for a stock with the following formula:

MCD:
Q4 2013 ROE_N = 35.72%
Q4 2013 BV= 16.16
P/E_3 = 17.62

$$P_1 = (BV * ROE_N) * P/E_3$$

Where:
P_1 = Price next period
BV = Book value per share
ROE_N = Normalized Return on Equity = $\frac{Net\ Income}{\frac{Equity_1 + Equity_2}{2}}$

P/E_3 = Average P/E over three years

$$P_1 = (16.16 * .3572) * 17.62 = \$101.71$$

Based on this simple valuation method, MCD is expected to be trading at $101.71 by the first quarter of 2014. The current stock price as of the fourth quarter of 2013 is $97.03. At the current price, MCD appears to be slightly undervalued. It is sometimes better to use a range of values for the inputs. This will give a high and low range of values for the price forecast.

There are many different price multiples that can be used for relative valuation purposes such as price to sales per share, price to cash flow per share, or any other fundamental value converted to a per share quantity can be used[6]. A relative valuation technique in conjunction with an absolute valuation method may give an investor a better idea of the true value of a company. When using absolute valuation methods, some tend to eliminate the possibility of finding companies in the same industry or sector that would provide a better return or

---

[6] For further study of relative valuation see Pinto et al (2010)

lower risk and the same holds true for relative valuation. It is possible to find companies that are a better value relative to other similar peer companies or a benchmark, but if the whole industry or peer companies under evaluation are overvalued on an absolute basis, it is possible to pay too much for a company. I hope Part II of this book has presented a basic understanding of how to value a company. If an investor has decided to actively manage a portfolio using individual stocks, this section of the book should provide a good primer for additional research into valuation methodology.

[PART III]

Portfolio Management

If an investor has decided that passive management is best suited for their investment expectations, then this is where they should continue their reading. Whether an active or passive investor, portfolio management it is extremely important in evaluating an entire portfolio. The previous chapters presented valuation formulas and possibly some investors have decided to pick individual stocks to construct their portfolios. If such is the case, the following chapters will be the most crucial in determining overall success or failure and has nothing to do with stock valuation. Portfolio management encompasses overall goals, the ability to take on risk, and an overall strategy that will guide investment decisions.

The following chapters will address the portfolio management process and discuss why this is so important. A passive investor's main focus will be on correlation between asset classes and diversification according to Modern Portfolio Theory or Capital Market Theory. As an active investor, diversification is of lesser value if picking individual stocks because the intention is to find value with best ideas, not the tenth best idea.

Active investing requires extreme discipline and a complete investment strategy that is modified only if absolutely necessary.

The first chapter will discuss the process for designing and implementing a portfolio investment policy statement. This is similar to any business process: plan, implement the plan, and monitor the progress of the plan that has been implemented. The Investment Policy Statement (IPS) is an invaluable tool for investors who want their assets invested in a certain way but want to hire a professional to implement it. While working with a financial advisor, keep in mind he or she may not have the knowledge or skill set to actually carry out an active IPS. The IPS is the foundation of portfolio management.

The next chapter will address the basics of passive portfolio management and capital market theory. A passive portfolio is designed to be low cost and low maintenance. I will explain the role of diversification in passive management as well as the role of the capital market line in determining the optimal portfolio for a passive investor.

Finally, the last chapter will turn the attention to active portfolio management. This chapter will address how to measure an active portfolio manager's abilities and whether the returns justify the risk the portfolio manager takes. If an investor decides to manage a portfolio using an active investment style, this chapter will help measure success.

The conclusion of portfolio management will address the Treynor/Black model in its most basic form and show a simple approach to using both a passive and active portfolio management style to take advantage of market inefficiencies in a nearly efficient market.

[7]

The Portfolio Management Process

I t seems that in today's myopic world, investors and advisors alike tend to overlook the basics in the portfolio management process. I have seen in my career, countless investors with assets scattered across many advisors using supposedly different strategies in an attempt to diversify a portfolio. This is almost diversifying the diversified. In today's fast paced world when investors or advisers forget the basics, they are often reminded harshly that the basics are there for a reason. This chapter addresses the most basic investment concept and the most important: the portfolio management process. This is the process for laying out goals and dreams and attempting to quantify risk tolerances and expectations. In this process, an investor develops his strategy, a step by step guide to how his money will be invested and managed for the of benefit today and in the future. This process is a circle that never ends; even after the investment plan is in place, investors must monitor it and adjust it as lifestyles and needs change. Before a dollar is invested whether passive or active, all investors should have an Investment Policy Statement (IPS) completed and a plan for how the IPS will be evaluated.

There are three basic steps in the portfolio management process:

1. Create the Investment Policy Statement
2. Develop and Implement the Investment Strategy
3. Evaluate the process and progress of the investment strategy and IPS

The IPS is the foundation of the investment process that explains in detail an investor's goals and constraints. It is here that investor's articulate expectations about returns and the level of risk they are willing and able to accept in an attempt to meet these expectations. Most people refer to an IPS as a method to place constraints and provide discipline to the portfolio manager, which can be the individual investor or a professional money manager. The IPS should be so detailed that any professional money manager should be able to pick up where the investor or a previous money manager left the account. The portfolio or investment strategy may differ but the IPS objectives remain the same.

The first thing we need to address are constraints. Are there liquidity needs such as monthly distributions or time horizon constraints that prevent investors from taking on additional risk? An investor's time horizon tends to dictate at least in part the ability to take risk. Some investors may psychologically be willing to accept additional risk, but due to time horizon issues are unable to do so without permanently damaging their ability to meet future investment and income requirements. It could be that tax concerns affect taking profits too early or even taking distribution at all. It is in this part of the process where investors or account managers clarify special circumstances or preferences that will alter the way a portfolio is managed.

Next, quantify return expectations based on the amount of risk the investor is willing and able to accept. Return objectives can be stated in several ways. Some investors want to state return objectives relative to a benchmark, while others want an absolute return such as 8%. I prefer absolute returns as opposed to relative returns since absolute returns are identifiable whereas relative performance can mean negative returns are expected and acceptable. For example if an account has a return objective of beating the S&P 500 index by 2% and the S&P 500 returns negative 20%, it is acceptable based on the IPS to return a negative 18%. It must be understood that a stated absolute return objective of 8% annually does not mean the portfolio will attain this goal year over year and that if it does not an investor should change strategies or fire his/her investment manager. If the account is unable to attain the IPS objective, investigate why it was unable to attain the goal and adjust the strategy accordingly. Investors may find that their account did not meet the investment objective, but due to the current investment environment, the goal was unattainable at their current level of risk.

Unfortunately most investors forego this step and move right on to the investment and asset allocation step. By skipping ahead many investors may not truly understand the level of risk they are taking or that they are setting a pace that is likely to disappoint in the future. Over the years I have noticed that without clear set goals outlined in an IPS, many investors become more aggressive and take on more risk when in a bull market. Doing this sets them up for failure in the future. When the markets turn bearish, only after substantial loses do they realize they are more risk adverse than when the market was moving higher. The IPS keeps the investor and the portfolio manager on track and helps minimize emotional based portfolio management.

So how does an investor quantify the risk he/she is willing or able to take? Finance uses the measure of risk based on the standard deviation of returns for the entire portfolio. The standard deviation measures the dispersion of returns or the volatility of returns on a single asset or an entire portfolio. The standard deviation (σ) is the square-root of an asset's variance (σ^2). I will try to minimize the use of formulas, but they are essential in understanding portfolio risk. The variance essentially measures the same thing as the standard deviation which is the volatility of an asset or portfolio. When looking at a single stock, the variance is the difference between the return in a given period and the mean return of the stock squared, divided by the number of periods.

$$\sigma^2 = \frac{\sum_{t=1}^{T}(Return_t - Mean\ return)^2}{Number\ of\ Periods}$$

The standard deviation of a stock is the square-root of the variance.

$$\sigma = \sqrt{\frac{\sum_{t=1}^{T}(Return_t - Mean\ return)^2}{Number\ of\ Periods}}$$

Most financial research websites will provide the standard deviation of returns for an individual stock. The equation for the standard deviation of a portfolio is where it gets a little cumbersome. The equation is not that difficult. It gets exponentially longer as assets are added to a portfolio. The standard deviation allows the quantification of the level of risk. For example, an investor can assess his/her level of risk by taking a risk tolerance questionnaire. Let us suppose they discover that that their account can handle a move in either direction by 10% which is a standard deviation of 10%. A portfolio managed to allow only a maximum loss of 10% in a given year is desirable. The above calculation is for an individual stock. To measure a portfolio's standard deviation, it is necessary to understand the relationship between two assets and how they move to-gether. This is known as covariance and from this an investor can determine the correlation between two assets. The covar-iance between asset *a* and asset *b* is:

Covariance = Σ (Return of a – Avg. Return of a) * Return of b – Avg. Return of b) / (number of periods-1)

For example, suppose we have the following return data on stock *a* and stock *b*.

Day	Stock *a* (%)	Stock *b* (%)
1	1	2
2	2	5
3	3	8
4	4	9

The mean return for Stock *a* is (1+2+3+4)/4 = 2.5
The mean return for Stock *b* is (2+5+8+9)/4 = 6
The covariance of returns =

Cov(a,b) = [(1-2.5) * (2-6)] + [(2-2.25) * (5-6)] + [(3-2.5) * (8-6)] + [(4-2.25) * (9-6)] / (4-1) = 4.00

Use the above standard deviation formula to calculate the standard deviation for both stock *a* and stock *b* to find that the standard deviation of stock *a* is:

$$\sigma_a = \sqrt{\frac{(1-2.5)^2 + (2-2.5)^2 + (3-2.5)^2 + (4-2.5)^2}{4}} = 1.29$$

The standard deviation of stock *b* is:

$$\sigma_a = \sqrt{\frac{(2-6)^2 + (5-6)^2 + (8-6)^2 + (9-6)^2}{4}} = 3.16$$

To calculate the correlation between two stocks, find the covariance and the standard deviation for both stocks. The correlation coefficient is:

$$\rho_{a,b,} = \frac{Cov_{a,b}}{\sigma_a \sigma_b}$$

So the correlation between Stock *a* and Stock *b* is:

$$\rho_{a,b,} = \frac{4}{1.29 * 3.16} = .9804$$

The correlation between Stock *a* and Stock *b* is .9804 which is nearly perfectly correlated. Correlation will always be between +1 and -1. A correlation coefficient of +1 means if Stock *a* goes up by one percent, Stock *b* will also go up by one percent. A correlation coefficient of -1 means if Stock *a* goes up by one percent, Stock *b* will go **down** by one percent. The correlation between assets plays a key role in diversification. Since standard deviation is not additive, risk can be measured in terms of a weighted average of standard deviation, the total risk of a portfolio is less than the sum of its parts.

Constructing a portfolio with 50% in asset a, and 50% in asset b, the portfolio's standard deviation would be 2.216%. The following formula is used to calculate a portfolio with only two stocks and can easily be expanded upon to add additional stocks.

$$\sigma_{Portfolio} = \sqrt{w_a^2 \sigma_a^2 + w_b^2 \sigma_b^2 + 2w_a w_b Cov(a,b)}$$

Where:
w = Weight of stock
$\sigma = Standard\ deviation\ of\ stock$
Cov(a,b)= Covariance between Stock a and Stock b

Arriving at this point was labor intensive, but it is important to understand how the risk of a portfolio is a combination of factors that can be separated and analyzed. From the above equation, the covariance is an important concept in portfolio risk. To reduce the risk of a portfolio, an investor would ulti-mately want the correlation between the two assets to be neg-ative. This would reduce the risk for the portfolio and is the main determinate in the concept of diversification and a staple in Modern Portfolio Theory and Capital Market Theory.

The next step is to determine investment objectives which are normally stated as expected returns. Stating the level of risk an investor is willing and able to accept makes it easier to man-age expectations regarding expected returns. Financial theory suggests investors cannot expect to earn higher returns with-out assuming additional risk. In the financial world this is known as the "risk-return trade-off." So if analyzing two dif-ferent stock portfolios, one has a standard deviation of 10% and an expected return of 15%, while the other has a standard de-viation of 20% and an expected return of 25%, investors cannot rationally expect to receive the return from the second portfolio while maintaining a risk tolerance of 10%. This is why it is important to understand risk tolerance before expecting high returns.

Armed with expectations of future market returns and a de-fined level of risk, it is time to decide on what style of investing to utilize. Is the best choice a passive portfolio strategy or an active portfolio strategy, or a mixture of both? The next two chapters present details regarding passive and active strate-gies. Passive investing can mean different things, but the

main definition is it does not attempt to outperform a benchmark. Its main goal is to mimic a benchmark such as the total
stock market. Indexing is a common form of passive management. Active management means an investor or a portfolio
manager hired by the investor will attempt to beat a benchmark. This attempt to gain excess returns is called adding alpha. For example, an investor was benchmarked to the S&P
500 which just returned 10% over the last year. If the investor
achieved 15% without taking on additional risk, the investor
would have earned excess returns of 5% or an alpha of 5%.

The constraints, risks and returns, and investment style of the
IPS have been presented. Now let us focus on the allocation
process which is often called strategic asset allocation. Strategic asset allocation involves deciding on which asset classes are
suitable for portfolios. For example, if a retired investor needs
a monthly systematic distribution from a portfolio, he or she
will have a liquidity requirement and avoid assets that are illiquid such as direct investment in real estate. Asset classes
can be divided and subdivided in to many different groups.
The three main broad asset classes are stock, bonds, and cash.
Each of these asset classes can be broken into subdividing asset classes such as small cap stocks and mid cap stocks while
bonds can be subdivided into government bonds and corporate
bonds. The asset classes subsequently need to be assigned a
weight or a range of weights. For example, suppose an appropriate allocation mix is 60% equities and 40% bonds. This could
subdivide the equities into 15% small cap equities, 15% mid
cap equities and 30% large cap equities as long as the risk and
return expectation are within our IPS acceptable range.

With the IPS clearly defined and ready to be implemented, the
investor has now reached the step that most investors jump to
when deciding to begin investing. This is the implementation
phase. In this phase either the investor or the portfolio manager begins selecting assets for the portfolio. The portfolio is

constantly being monitored and reviewed by the manager and any changes to the investor's circumstance or expectations about future market risk and returns will determine whether the portfolio will need to be revised. This is the last step of the portfolio management process and is called the monitoring and feedback step.

Armed with an understanding of how to draft and implement an IPS, an investor or account manager needs to turn his/her attention to the differences in investment style. This is a crucial component to managing expectations. If investors decide to hire a professional portfolio manager, they often take the advice of the professional regarding whether to use active or passive portfolio management. Recall from the chapter on behavioral finance that most tend to believe first and ask question later. This is potentially devastating to investors regarding the active versus passive decision. After a comprehensive understanding of the information in the chapters on passive and active investing, investors will be able to make an educated decision and form an educated opinion on how assets can and should be managed.

[8]

The Concept of Utility

I want to take a little detour here and explain Utility functions for the investor and for the advisor who wishes to better understand the concept of rational investor decisions. Risk and utility functions have been a topic that has been relatively difficult for me to comprehend in such a way that I can eloquently explain it. Utility functions are used in both active and passive investing. Risk aversion, λ, is linked to expected utility through the following equation:

$$E(U)= \varsigma_p - \lambda_T * \sigma_p^2$$

Where:
E(U) is the Expected Utility
ς_p = Expected Excess Returns on the Portfolio
σ_p^2 = Variance of Return on the Portfolio
λ_T = Total Risk Aversion

The concept of Total Risk Aversion will be addressed in the chapter on active portfolio management. For now I will try to explain expected utility in a way investors can easily understand. Total risk aversion is directly tied to utility and can be rather difficult to grasp. Since individual investors will likely

have different levels of risk aversion, I will do my best to explain this concept.

One of the greatest explanations for utility was an experiment
conducted by Nicholas Bernoulli in the 1700s and has been
named the St. Petersburg Paradox. This experiment is most
easily understood with an example. I am going to flip a coin
and if it lands on heads, I will pay $1. I will flip the coin again
and if it lands on heads again, I will give $2. I will double the
winnings each time until it lands on tails. Once it lands on
tails, it is over. If it lands on heads the first time and the next
time it lands on tails, the game is over. So to sum it up, I will
flip a coin, and as long as it lands on heads, I will double the
winnings paid out. When it lands on tails for the first time,
the game stops. How much would someone pay to play this
game? Now I will play the same game but start with $1000.
How much would someone pay to play now? Most people
would not take into consideration the possibility of winning an
infinite amount of money. Most minds likely stop at the first
coin flip. If I win a dollar, but the next flip is tails, I will only
get one dollar and if I wager more than that I have a chance to
lose money. This is typical of most investors and plays directly
into the hands of diminishing marginal utility of wealth.
Chalk up a point for the theory of risk aversion. If investments
were risk neutral, investors or account managers would all accept a fair bet or gamble. In other words, risk neutral investors
would be willing to pay $30 for a 30% chance of winning $100
even though they still have a 70% chance of winning nothing.
The challenge I have come to accept with expected utility is
that I would need to observe each individual to determine the
value they put on their investments, or their unique utility. As
demonstrated with the St. Petersburg Paradox experiment, investors are likely to pay less than the $30 for a chance at win-
ning $100. Bernoulli's concepts of utility are far reaching and
have been used to explain why poor people will pay a premium

to transfer risk and why rich people will take the risk in exchange for the premium. Hence the concept of Insurance. Bernoulli was a pioneer in the field of psychophysics even before the term was invented. He observed people making decisions that confirm what is now known as risk aversion. He noticed that if given the choice between a gamble and a guaranteed amount equal to the expected value of the gamble, the person would choose the guaranteed amount. This aversion to risk is central to Modern Portfolio Theory.

Economists have devised ways to quantify expected utility by observing the choices investors make. Paul Samuelson revealed this relative utility by observing people's willingness to pay and explains it ever so eloquently:

> Utility is taken to be correlative to Desire or Want. It has been already argued that desires cannot be measured directly, but only indirectly, by the outward phenomena to which they give rise: and that in those cases with which economics is chiefly concerned the measure is found in the price which a person is willing to pay for the fulfillment or satisfaction of his desire.

Consider an investor with a logarithmic utility function. Since a negative number cannot have an accurate log, assume this investment has two positive outcomes and are equally likely. In this particular venture, the investors can make either $1 or $1000 dollars. Of course an investor would desire to earn the $1000 dollars and would not want to earn only $1. The expected value of this investment is:

Expected Value (EV) = 0.5 * $1 + 0.5 * $1000 = $500.50

Since this a log utility, take the natural log of the expected value in order to turn this into units.

EV of Utility = ln($500.50) = 6.216 Units

Most investors are risk adverse, and the utility for the invest-ment since it has an element of risk involved will be lower than a guarantee for the expected value of $500.50. To calculate the units involved when risk is introduced to the equation is:

(EV) of Utility of the Investment = 0.5 * ln($1) +0.5 * ln($1000) = 3.4538 Units

I will introduce a new term here called certainty equivalents. This is the guaranteed value of an investment that this inves-tor would accept rather than take a chance to receive more money but is faced with uncertainty in receiving the higher in-vestment amount. Certainty equivalents give an intuitive way of thinking about risk as well as a way to think about investor's risk aversion. In this example the investor's certainty equiva-lent is equal to:

(EV) of Certainty Equivalent Utility = ln(x) = 3.4538 units

Using algebra and solving for "x,' the result is a certainty equivalent of $31.62. So, if the expected value was $500.50 compared to the $31.62, there is a rather high risk premium. An investor would need to be compensated $468.88 above the cash equivalent in order to take on the risk of uncertainty. The certainty equivalent is saying that this investor is indifferent about taking the $31.62 which is certain and taking on the risk of receiving $1 or $1000. The narrower the gap between the rewards on the investment the smaller the risk premium.

Let us assume we quantify the risk aversion parameter and use a scale of 0-2.5 for investors who have a low degree of risk aversion and 2.51 to 5.5 for investors with a moderate degree of risk aversion, and 5.56 to 9 for investors with a high degree of risk aversion. Now assume an account manager is meeting with a client whom has been assessed and can be assigned a quantified risk aversion parameter of 5. The manager must choose between two portfolios, Portfolio A and Portfolio B. Portfolio A and B have the following characteristics:

Portfolio A: Expected return of 10% and a standard deviation of 20%

Portfolio B: Expected return of 7% and a standard deviation of 12%.

Which portfolio should be selected for the client? The expected utility equation for a mean/variance portfolio is:

$$U_P = E(R_P) - 0.005\lambda_T\sigma_P^2$$

Where:
U_P = Utility of Portfolio
$E(R_P)$ = Expected Return of Portfolio
λ_T = Investors Risk Aversion
σ_P^2 = Variance of Return of Portfolio

The risk-adjusted (expected utility) expected return for portfolio A is 0 found by U_P= 10 - .025(400). The risk-adjusted expected return for portfolio B is 3.4% found by U_P = 7 - .025(144).

Therefore the client who has a quantified risk aversion of 5 and based on the scale would choose Portfolio B as opposed to Portfolio A.

Often clients will look at the expected return and not fully understand the risk involved in pursuing that return. It is the advisor's job to steer clients in the right direction. For advisors who have had as difficult a time as I have in grasping the quantitative side of expected utility, I hope this helps and will make it possible to take something away from it and explain it to clients.

Now with some clarity regarding expected utility which is generally related to rational investment decisions of risk averse investors and directly relates to Modern Portfolio Theory and passive portfolio management, let us look at irrational investors.

Daniel Kahnman and Amos Tversky's Prospect Theory disagrees with expected utility theory on at least two fronts. First is the concept of a reference point. Expected Utility Theory believes that reference points are irrelevant, and the utility of a person's wealth is what makes them happy. If this were true and an investor had ten million dollars today as did a best friend, utility theory would postulate that both would have the same utility. However, if that same investor had twenty million dollars the day before and the best friend had only five million dollars, would each still have the same utility of wealth? Kahneman and Tversky think not. Without a reference point, Utility Theory misses the fact that when faced with a possible loss or a guaranteed loss, most investors do not behave in a risk adverse manner but rather in a risk seeking manner. Consider an example.

Suppose an individual has a current wealth of $5 million and has the choice between a gamble versus a guarantee.

The gamble: a 50% chance of an ending wealth of $1 million or a 50% change of $5 million

The guarantee: an ending wealth value of $3 million.

Which of the above would an investor choose? The gamble or the guarantee? Most would choose the gamble: taking a chance at maintaining a current level of wealth as opposed to guaranteeing a lower level of wealth. This scenario moves in the opposite direction of Utility Theory and actually is risk seeking instead of risk adverse. There is a 50% chance of decreasing our wealth to $1 million. In fact the expected value of each scenario is $3 million. According to expected utility theory, a rational decision maker would have taken the guaranteed loss of $2 million.

Expected utility states that humans are good at assessing probabilities and tend to make rational decisions. Prospect theory disagrees and states that humans tend to be horrible at probability weightings and often make wrong decisions when confronted with alternative investments with different weightings. Recall the behavioral bias of loss aversion where people tend to find losing money about twice as agonizing as gaining the equivalent amount of money. This brings up another situation. Investors must decide which to believe as the most accurate regarding how investors make decision which refers to the question of whether investors are rational or irrational, and are markets efficient or inefficient. It is tough I know.

I must mention one more detail that may or may not help in a decision regarding whether investors are rational or irrational. Markowitz claims the appearance of irrationality in prospect theory can be described using Weber's law. Weber's law is the minimum difference in stimulation that a person can detect 50% of the time. This means that the amount of stimuli that is detectible is proportional to the base level, or amount if considering money. An example: if a customer goes to computer store and buys a computer for $500 and is offered additional upgrades for $200, most will probably stop and think before agreeing since the upgrades cost nearly half of what the computer cost. However, if a customer goes to a car dealership and buys a $50,000 car and is offered upgrades for $200, most will likely not think twice since the $200 is small in comparison to $50,000. Weber's law is based on a constant proportion as opposed to a constant amount. So Markowitz argues that at times investors may make irrational decision regarding pennies but will make rational decisions regarding tens of thousands of dollars.

I hope this explanation offers more clarity. There are thousands of books on specific ways to invest, but most only tell one side of the story which leads not only to false feelings of security but to potentially disastrous investing results. Remember that so far I have presented theory and not reality in all of the above examples. In investing the outcomes are not known, so it would be difficult to be put in a situation that would require a choice between two guaranteed losses. I would say that Expected Utility Theory has flaws and is not infallibly accurate but can be helpful in portfolio selection and management.

[9]

Passive Portfolio Management

Passive investing is often thought of as simply a buy and hold strategy that is very simple to implement. While a passive strategy is easier to implement than an active strategy, it is far from picking a few mutual funds and letting them sit until retirement or until the funds are needed. Investors still need to do homework which is what this chapter is dedicated toward. As I mentioned before, even if an investor believes in active management and the markets inefficiencies, he or she may still not be able to implement a proper active strategy. On the other hand, if an investor believes that markets are efficient and most are unable to beat the market for extended periods of time, then they would default to a passive strategy. Either way this chapter should serve as a guide in constructing a passively managed portfolio.

Harry Markowitz is considered the father of Modern Portfolio Theory (MPT) based on his Nobel Prize winning paper describing optimal portfolios as those that are mean/variance optimized. Markowitz wanted it to be understood that mean-variance analysis was to be applied to a portfolio, not necessarily to individual securities. The cornerstone of MPT is the concept of diversification. After the latest financial crisis of 2008 when most asset classes became highly correlated on the downside, many scholars and financial professionals began scrutinizing MPT claiming that it has failed and only works if return distributions are normal. He has called the period "The Great Confusion." Mr. Markowitz has proven in his book *Portfolio Selection,* that he never claimed or required a normal distribution for MPT to work and that it will work in all market environments even non-normal markets. Markowitz claims that most investors can be described with a utility curve that is concave, which means they are risk-adverse, as opposed to a convex utility curve that implies the investor is risk seeking. Many in opposition to Markowitz's theory assert that mean-variance efficient portfolios will only give optimal expected utility if return distributions are normal and the utility is quadratic. The statisticians who reject Markowitz's hypothesis do so because they believe return distributions are not normal and any concave quadratic will reach a maximum level before turning and eventually moving in the wrong direction. As with anyone who is defending life-long work, Markowitz has shown that a portfolio with returns that are between a 30% loss and a 40% gain there is little difference between the expected utility and the quadratic. For a more in-depth discussion regarding mean-variance analysis, refer to Markowitz's new book *Risk-Return Analysis Volume one.*

Markowitz explains that MPT assumes that investors are rational based on the expected utility maxim. The expected utility maxim in its most basic form states that a rational investor will prefer less risk to more given the same expected return. As discusses in previous chapters on human behavior regarding decisions when the outcome is not known, it appears that humans are often irrational in their decision making and numerous examples have been given by Tversky and Kahneman. The previous chapter demonstrated how Markowitz disproves irrational behaviors using Weber's Law, so this chapter regarding passive investing will assume Markowitz is correct and as demonstrated in the following paragraphs, the CAPM

shows that the efficient portfolio is the portfolio that encompasses the entire stock market.

Recall from Chapter 4 the discussion regarding the CAPM and
expected returns and their use in stock valuation. The main
concept discussed within this model was beta and its relation
to the concept of portfolio and stock volatility or risk. A stock
or portfolio's beta allows for the separation of risk between
market risk and residual risk. Residual risk is the risk in excess of the markets risks.

$$\omega_P^2 = \beta_P^2 \sigma_M^2 - \sigma_P^2 \ [7]$$

Where:
ω_P^2 = Residual variance
σ_P^2 = Portfolio Variance
$\beta_P^2 \sigma_M^2$ = Portfolio Variance related to market

Even though it was concluded that CAPM was a poor predictor
of expected returns, it is not easy to ignore. CAPM is a passive
portfolio investor's best friend. Since a stock or portfolio's excess return is proportional to its beta, it cannot have a residual
excess return which means a portfolio of stocks must have an
expected residual return of zero. If a stock or portfolio is unable to provide residual return, the optimal portfolio would be
the portfolio with no residual risk and a beta of one which is
equal to the market portfolio. The CAPM underlying assumption is that investors are rewarded for taking "necessary" risk,
but any risk above necessary is, well, unnecessary, and the investor is at fault for adding the additional risk. This may be a
little confusing so here is a simplified example. If investor X
has constructed a portfolio that differs from the market and
has residual risk while investor Y has constructed a portfolio
that is equal to the market, but does not have residual risk?

---

[7] See Grinold and Kahn (1999)

The markets are constructed in a way that for every buyer of a stock there has to be a seller. So after every transaction, there will eventually be a winner and a loser. If Investor X has constructed a portfolio with residual returns that are positive, there must be an investor, investor W who has constructed a portfolio with residual risk opposite that of investor X and would have a negative residual return. The passive investing community calls this the zero-sum game. Why would anyone increase the amount of risk without an increase in return? If CAPM's assumptions are correct and there are no residual returns available to those that deviate from the market, the market portfolio is then the optimal portfolio. This argument should cause investors to consider passive portfolio management. It is best for an investor to be honest with themselves at this juncture and truly assess their ability to be Investor X.

How can an investor or adviser construct an optimal passive portfolio? First remember that there is not a perfect way to construct an optimal portfolio in the real world; the purpose is to get as close to optimal as possible. Think back to the chapter on behavior finance and recall the biases for mental accounting and loss aversion. I want to explain something here because I feel it is likely the most important concept of this chapter. Let us look at mental accounting first as it pertains to portfolio construction. Recall that a mental account is when an investor keeps track of individual accounts or even individual positions within accounts as opposed to taking a comprehensive view of the entire portfolio. As a steward of client assets, it is useful to attempt to determine which clients exhibit this bias and help them deal with the mental accounting by setting up different accounts based on risk or needs. It is best to set up an account that is safe such as money markets or short-term government debt that the client will understand as being safe and used for liquidity. The account manager can build another portfolio that is designed to hold the riskier investment for long-term growth. Managers who are able to build portfolios for different purposes will notice that the mental accounting will at least be calmed with these clients. Since investors can have a difficult time seeing individual positions in a comprehensive manner, the advisor can construct individual accounts with different purposes and allow the client to keep track of each account based on the objective of the account.

As an independent investor, it may be difficult to notice the damage to an overall investment strategy due to the effects of mental accounting. For investors managing their own money, I recommend separating accounts based on risk and expected return.

Second, loss aversion is a behavioral bias that is easier for an advisor to spot in clients than it is for individual investors to spot in themselves. Recall that loss aversion will cause an investor to take on more risk when confronted with a probability scenario of which one outcome is a large loss. What does this have to do with implementing a passive strategy? Whether an advisor managing client assets or an investor managing his or her own assets, the decision making process will likely have the largest impact on investments over any other single factor. I hope I have clarified the importance of designing investment strategies around potential short comings. Behavioral biases should cause investors to think about how to handle the asset allocation component of a portfolio. Modern Portfolio Theory gives an easy to follow guide to build an optimized portfolio, but why do so many investors fail upon execution? The cause is likely the biases mention above and the others discussed in the behavioral finance chapter. If the biases can be addressed or at least identified, it should be possible to structure a passive portfolio that is successful over the long-term.

An investor can start by taking a strategic approach to asset allocation. Asset allocation is used in both passive and active management. Investors can think of passive management as taking a long-term view of capital markets and matching their risk tolerance with their return expectations. Markowitz's Theory states that the market portfolio is the optimal risky portfolio. Investors need to adjust this optimal risky portfolio to address their investor biases and their risk tolerance. If we can do this we can successfully implement a passive strategy. Strategic Asset Allocation is a key component of MPT. It is used to match a portfolio's riskiness to that of an investor's.

The number one objective of utilizing a passive portfolio strategy is to maximize return while minimizing risk. The only inputs needed for a mean-variance analysis are the means, variances, and co-variances of the assets. The ideal way to construct a passive portfolio is to use mean-variance minimizing software. Discussed in the previous chapter were the concept of correlation, covariance, and standard deviation. In the world of investments, there are thousands of investments to choose from and knowing which to include in a portfolio can be an overwhelming task. We know that investors want assets with low correlation included in their investment universe as assets with high correlation don't add much diversification or bang for their buck so to speak.

The plan is to build a portfolio with the highest expected return for the lowest amount of risk. The first thing to do is define the universe. For a passive investment strategy, I would recommend ETFs that are indexed to a benchmark as they tend to have extremely low expense ratios and maintain proper benchmark exposure. Debates still remain as to the proper asset classes to add to a portfolio for proper diversification. Some will say a total stock market ETF will suffice while another would say there is a need to break up a portfolio in to several subsectors such as energy and real estate. It is up to the investor as to how many asset classes they want to keep track of and monitor. I personally would choose a few ETFs to represent the stock market as a whole, which would likely consist of one for U.S. stocks, one for International stocks, and one for emerging market stocks. I would do the same for the fixed income market. If investors do not want to purchase software to calculate the lowest mean-variance portfolio, the same guides are available on the internet to show the steps to build one in excel.

Once the investment universe has been identified, calculate the average return and standard deviation over a specified time frame such as five years or use a complete business cycle for the time frame. A wise investor wants to get a feel for the investments to be purchased. If choosing a short period to calculate average returns, there is a possibility to under or overestimate the volatility within these return data or completely misrepresent the return structure for the investments. I would recommend at a minimum five years of historical return data. In analyzing return data, it is possible to notice that certain asset classes show extremely high returns in certain periods during the business cycle and there may be a need to adjust the return data up or down depending on the findings.

Once comfortable with average return data, it is time to build a covariance matrix. This is when it is critical to have software to calculate the covariance for each pair of investments. If building an Excel spreadsheet, add weights to all columns and rows and make sure they sum to one. At this point, there should be three separate tables, one for expected returns, one with the covariance matrix, and one with the portfolio statistics. The portfolio statistics should consist of the portfolio average return and the standard deviation of portfolio returns. Once this data has been entered in Excel, use the Excel solver function to calculate the lowest possible standard deviation with the set of investment options available. I will not go into detail on how to build the Excel spreadsheet as there are numerous instructional sources on the Internet. The key point here is that passive investing involves creating a portfolio that

minimizes the risk of owning a single investment while max‑
imizing the returns based on this risk level.

An investor can simplify the above procedures by using only
two securities, Security A and Security B, to build out an effi‑
cient frontier. Here is an example of the entire procedure to
present a basic understanding as to what is being accom‑
plished.

Assume Security A has average or expected returns of 10% and
a standard deviation 20%. Security B has expected returns of
20% with a standard deviation of 30%. Assume both are neg‑
atively correlated with a correlation coefficient of ‑.02.

	Security A	Security B
Expected Returns	10%	20%
Standard Deviation	20%	30%
Correlation	‑0.2	

Figure: 9.1

Next, combine these two assets to form a portfolio. The key to
building the efficient frontier is the weights allocated to each
asset so that the portfolio will have minimum risk with the
highest return. In theory an investor can create an infinite
number of portfolios by adjusting the weights; however, for the
purpose of this example I will plot the efficient frontier in
larger increments. To calculate the expected portfolio return
when each security is equally weighted (i.e. 50% in each asset),
use the following formula:

Expected Return = 0.5*10% + .05*20% = 15%

Standard Deviation =

$$\sigma_{Portfolio} = \sqrt{(.5_a^2 * .20_a^2) + (.5_b^2 * .30_b^2) + 2(-.2) * .5_a * 5 * .2 * .3)} = 16\%$$

Where:
w = Weight of stock
σ = *Standard deviation of stock*
Cov(a,b) = Covariance between Stock a and Stock b

Portfolio	Wgt of A	Wgt of B	Expected Return of Portfolio	Standard Deviation of Portfolio
1	1	0	10%	20%
2	0.9	0.1	11%	18%
3	0.75	0.25	13%	15%
4	0.5	0.5	15%	16%
5	0.25	0.75	18%	22%
6	0	1	20%	30%

Figure 9.3

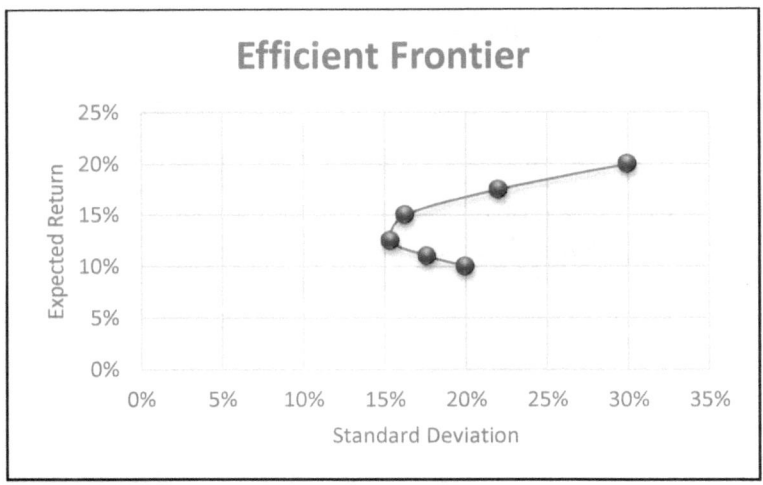

Figure 9.2

This example illustrates how an efficient portfolio of risky assets is allocated in order to create optimal portfolios. Now let us consider adding a risk free asset such as a government bond. There are investors who are risk adverse to the point that even an optimal portfolio with the lowest standard deviation will not satisfy their need for safety. Introducing a risk free asset to the equation can lower risk beyond what it is capable of with an optimal portfolio. The risk free asset has a standard deviation of zero and a correlation the risky portfolio of zero because all returns are known. To calculate the expected return for a portfolio with a weighting in a risk-free asset, use the following formula:

$$ER_p = (1 - w_T)R_F + w_T E(R_T)$$

Where:
ER_p = Expected Return on the Portfolio
(w_T) = Proportion of asset or weight
R_F = Risk-free Return
$E(R_T)$ = Expected Return on the Tangent Portfolio

The tangent portfolio, is the point where the risk-free asset is tangent to the efficient frontier of optimal risky assets as shown in Figure 9.4. It is also possible to calculate the standard deviation of the portfolio as:

$$\sigma_p = \sqrt{[(1 - w_T)^2 \sigma_{RF}^2 + w_T^2 \sigma_{RT}^2 + 2(1 - w_T)w_T \sigma_{RF} \sigma_{RT} \rho_{RF,RT}]}$$

The equation above looks rather scary but recall that the risk free asset has a standard deviation of zero and a correlation to the risky portfolio of zero, so the above equation simplifies to:

$$\sigma_P = w_T \sigma_{RT}$$

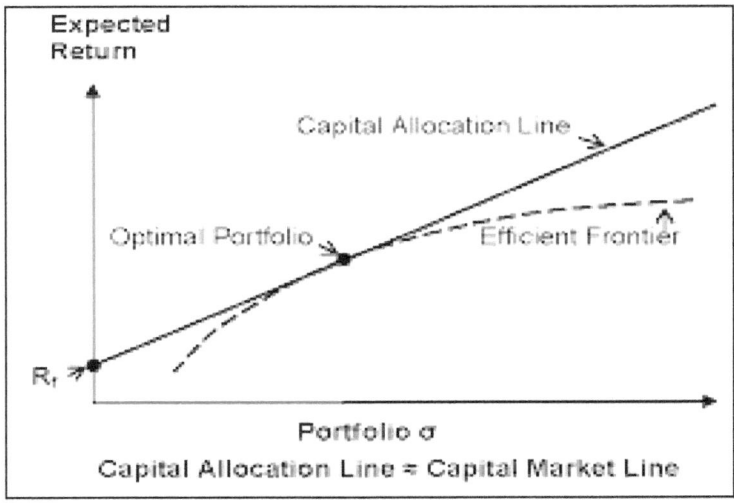

Figure 9.4

Use the above equations to solve for the weight an investor would need to allocate to the risk-free asset to obtain a certain level of risk/standard deviation. Suppose the rate on a risk-free asset is 3% and the known expected return on an investor's tangency portfolio, $E(R_T)$, is 10% and a standard deviation of 18%. Create a portfolio with a standard deviation of 8%. How much would be needed to allocate to the risk-free asset and how much would be needed to allocate to the tangency portfolio? To solve this rearrange the formula from above to solve for the weight needed to allocate to the tangency portfolio instead of the standard deviation.

$$w_T = \frac{\sigma_P}{\sigma_{RT}}$$

The weight necessary to allocate to the tangency portfolio would be 44%, $(0.08/0.18 = .444)$. Then allocate 56% to the risk-free asset in order to create a portfolio with a standard deviation of 8%. Knowledge of the weights for the portfolio determines the expected return of the portfolio using the equation:

$$ER_p = (1 - w_T)R_F + w_T E(R_T)$$

The expected return, ER_p, for a portfolio with a standard deviation of 8% is roughly 6%.

An investor reading this is probably thinking, "There has to be a simpler method for passive investing." I have found that most passive investors do not think it is necessary to build out efficient frontiers. Most passive investors attempt to quantify the risk by determining a stock to bond ratio. This is a crude method, and I am sad to inform that most financial advisors typically give an investor a risk tolerance questionnaire that asks questions regarding risk. They add up the answers to receive a score that tells the advisor how much stock exposure the investor can handle. This is the less scientific way of obtaining an optimal portfolio.

Typical passive investors try to mimic the entire investable universe by purchasing low cost ETFs which is a personal decision. With the advent of ETFs that track an index, investors have been able to get the market's return without building ef-

ficient frontiers from a universe of individual stocks. For example, if an investor wants the return of the S&P 500 index,
he or she could buy the SPY ETF as opposed purchasing 500
individual stocks. This obviously will lower the investor's
transaction cost.

Look back at the discussion about the CAPM and remember
that CAPM tells investors that the optimal risky portfolio is
the "Market Portfolio" or the portfolio that represents all risky
assets. Since the efficient frontier the investor is trying to create is an optimal portfolio that provides the maximum return
for a given level of risk and the risk of a portfolio is made up of
both systematic (market risk) and unsystematic risk (stock
specific or diversifiable risk), it is possible to diversify away
unsystematic risk by adding additional assets to the portfolio.
The only way to have a completely diversified portfolio is to
own all risky assets since each additional asset introduced into
the portfolio further diversifies the portfolio.

A great example of an ETF that attempts to represent the entire stock market is Vanguard's Total Stock Market ETF,
which owns over 3,700 stocks based on market cap. In the financial advisory world, I often come across individuals who
own several ETFs ranging from the S&P 500 to the energy sector to real estate. As previously discussed, if an investor owns
an ETF that attempts to track the entire stock market, there
is no need to own additional ETFs that are indexed to different
sectors since the investor likely already owns the stocks within
that sector in the total stock market ETF and thereby adding
transaction cost and over diversifying. Look at an example. If
it is decided that the S&P 500 represents the entire stock market, it is assumed that the S&P 500 index is "the market."
Adding an additional asset class such as an ETF that represents the energy sector has added additional risk to the portfolio without increasing a return sufficient to justify adding the
position. To properly construct a passive portfolio without

having to spend hours building Excel spreadsheets and pour-ing over covariance matrixes, investors can purchase ETFs for different markets. This too is a personal decision as to what each investor is comfortable holding within a portfolio. If an investor wants to diversify domestically or internationally, there are ETFs that represent the world and ETFs that repre-sent a specific country's stock market. I typically see investors allocate within broad regions as opposed to owning specific countries. A passive investor will likely want to be invested in emerging markets as a whole as opposed to investing in indi-vidual countries that represent the emerging markets, such as Brazil, Russia, and China. Some passive investors do not want international exposure and opt to buy only domestic ETFs.

Before moving from this chapter, consider the exploration of real world options for designing and implementing a passive portfolio. Previous chapters have discussed all the building blocks for passive management and dabbled in the mathemat-ics behind it. Now is the time to build a step by step guide to implementing the strategy.

First it is important to identify the type of investor. This could be done by talking with an advisor or taking both a risk toler-ance questionnaire and behavioral decision making question-naire to determine an investor's profile. Assume people in general suffer from mental accounting and have a relatively moderate tolerance for risk which equates to a total risk toler-ance of around 12%. Next use portfolio optimizing software to determine how much to invest in each asset class based on ex-pectations for market returns and overall total risk tolerance. Additionally recall that most suffer from loss aversion and find it difficult to sustain large losses even if only temporary. It is critical to identify constraints and biases and incorporate those in an IPS. Most investors have a tendency to be rather harsh on themselves due to mental accounting and will set up three separate accounts. The first account will be the money needed now or in the near term. Some may decide to buy property or another asset and need the cash to be relatively riskless. This will be invested in short-term government bonds that can be purchased through an ETF that specializes in short-term government debt.

Now that it has been decided that in order to diversify away most of the systematic risk we only need to invest in ETFs that represent the broad market, small capitalization stocks, mid-capitalization stocks and large-capitalization stocks. We do not want any foreign exposure. We then focus on our fixed income portfolio and strategically decide to focus on corporate debt, high yield debt, and government debt.

At this point, it is important to run the portfolio optimization software and let us assume the allocation of the portfolio should be:

10% Small-capitalization stocks
20% Mid-capitalization stocks
30% Large-capitalization stocks

10% High Yield Bonds
10% Corporate Bonds
20% Government Bonds

Assume this portfolio falls within the preferred investment guidelines. An investor may have a difficult time sticking with the overall allocation in times of market volatility due to loss aversion and mental accounting. Therefore, stick to the plan and split the portfolio into an account labeled high risk and high return and another account labeled the core portfolio. The known high risk, high return account will be more risky and volatile than other components but will keep the investor focused on the previously established goals. The investor will split the accounts and allocate in the following manner.

High Risk- High Return:
10% Small-capitalization
10% Mid-Capitalization
10% High-Yield Bonds
5% Corporate Bonds

Core Portfolio:
10% Mid-capitalization stocks
30% Large-capitalization stocks
5% Corporate Bonds
20% Government Bonds

Attempting to split the accounts based on total risk will eliminate the necessity of separate asset allocation portfolios with separate risk and return parameters. When an investor builds multiple portfolios that are based on different risk and return objectives, the account can create an environment where the correlation between each portfolio is not taken into consideration, and the investor inadvertently has overlapping portfolios. If an investor creates an optimized portfolio based on their overall risk-return objectives and split the portfolio into portfolios that are labeled high risk and know that they will be more risky but are also likely to add the most return to their portfolio over time, they may be more likely to stick to their investment objectives. A single comprehensive portfolio that combines market fluctuation with behavioral biases may cause difficulty maintaining a passive portfolio allocation through a severe market downturn.

Consider an example that is representative of the real world. An investor could have easily built a portfolio based off a risk tolerance questionnaire that described that investor as a 60% equity and 40% fixed income investor. With no way of optimizing, it is possible to have invested in as little as two ETFs: 60% in a broad market equity ETF and 40% in a total bond market ETF.

The main lesson from passive investing is that the investor is not attempting to beat a specific index or benchmark, only trying to match the returns. This takes much of the guess work out of investing. By believing that markets are efficient or that an investor is unable to outperform the market because of lack of time or lack of skill, that same investor is no longer at the mercy of emotions. At least that is what a passive investor hopes. Time and time again passive investors prove that a sustained bear market is more than most can bear. As with any "rational" human being, most tend to want to be passive investors during a bull market and active investors during a bear market. The sad thing is most lack the skill to determine when a market has entered either a bear or bull market and whether it will continue or reverse. Recall from the chapter on behavioral investing that emotions will often lead to making the wrong decision at the wrong time. Therefore, if investors are able to control fear and greed and truly invest assets passively over several years, most will do fine. However, if an investor believes it is possible to avoid market meltdowns whether it is based on technical analysis or fundamentals and also believes it is possible to outperform a benchmark overtime, they should proceed to the next chapter.

[10]

Active Portfolio Management

In the early days, portfolio management was considered an art. Before there were computers to crunch massive amounts of data, portfolio managers used intuition and experience as a methodology to pick stocks and manage client portfolios. Today this art form is a science, whereby a portfolio manager uses structured analysis to manage a portfolio. The previous chapter addressed passive portfolio management, and this chapter should help determine individual capabilities of managing a portfolio. Some may want to be an active manager but are incapable of managing in such a way and will seek professional help. This chapter will help potential investors distinguish between a true portfolio manager and a financial salesman. This chapter should provide an investor with knowledge about speaking with a professional money manager and knowing the tough questions to ask before making a decision of who to trust with their assets.

This section takes a quantitative view of portfolio management which is similar to passive portfolio management when using mean/variance analysis. The chapter on passive portfolio management was concerned with total return and total risk. In active portfolio management, the concern is with the residual return and residual risk when attempting to outperform a benchmark.

Active portfolio management has one objective: to maximize the value-added from residual return. The value-added equation given in *Active Portfolio Management* by Grinold and Kahn is:

$$VA[P] = \alpha_P - \lambda_R * \omega_P^2$$

Where:
VA[P] = Value added to the Portfolio
$\alpha_P = Residual\ Return\ to\ the\ Portfolio$
$\lambda_R = Aversion\ to\ Residual\ Risk$
$\omega_P^2 = Variance\ of\ Residual\ Return$

The residual return on a portfolio, α_P, is the return that is uncorrelated to the benchmark return for which the active strategy is attempting to outperform. Financial advisors and investors often refer to residual return by the Greek letter representing it, Alpha. Note that from the linear regression equation that alpha is in fact uncorrelated to the benchmark return.

$$r_P(t) = \alpha_P + \beta_P r_B(t)$$

Where:
$r_P(t)$= Return on the Portfolio
α_P= Residual Return on the Portfolio
β_P= Beta of the Portfolio
$r_B(t)$= Return on the Benchmark

This equation is very similar to the CAPM equation:

$$E(r)_p = r_f + \beta_p(r_m - r_f)$$

Where:
$E(r)_p$= Expected Return of a Portfolio
r_f= Risk-Free Rate of Return

β_p= Beta of the Portfolio
r_m= Return on the Market

The difference between the active equation and the passive equation is obvious. The CAPM equation uses the risk-free rate in place of the residual return used in the active strategy. This shows the assumptions behind each equation. The use of the risk-free rate of return in the CAPM equation shows CAPM's assumption that markets are in equilibrium. The use of alpha in the equation for active management demonstrates that a portfolio has returns above the benchmark that are not correlated with the returns of the benchmark. The term $(\beta_p r_B(t))$ is the correlated return of a portfolio to the benchmark. The beta of a portfolio as discussed in previous chapters is the covariance between the portfolio and the market/benchmark divided by the variance of returns for the market/benchmark.

$$\beta_p = \frac{Cov(p, m)}{\sigma_m^2}$$

Where:
$Cov(p, m)$= Covariance between the portfolio and the market
σ_m^2= Variance of the Market

When the beta of a portfolio is multiplied by the return of the market we get the return that is due to the move in the market whether it is up or down. Alpha is the "left over" portion of the equation.

The next logical question is, how does an investor go about seeking alpha for her active portfolio? Investors know that when they look at a stock price today, they can assume markets have efficiently priced the stock based on current market conditions and available information. So they can attempt to forecast alpha using valuation. Let us assume they have decided to use the dividend discount model in an attempt to find alpha. Refer back to the chapters on valuation to refresh your-self on the formulas and concepts.

Consider analyzing a stock with the following characteristics:

Current Price: $20
Dividend: $1
Dividend Growth forever: 10%
Required Rate of Return (using CAPM): 15%

Recall the Gordon Constant Growth Rate model as:

$$V_0 = \frac{D_1}{r - g}$$

The above information results in a present value price of $22.

$$V_0 = \frac{1.10}{.15 - .10} = 22$$

Conclude that the market is undervaluing this stock by $2 which is a forecasted residual return or alpha of 10%.

Assume that the standard deviation of a residual return is 20%. This would imply that the expected price of $22 versus the market price of the stock over the time period moved up or down 20% versus its average.

Two vital pieces of information are used by investors to deter-mine how well they are or their portfolio manager is efficiently using information to obtain alpha. If the investor takes a re-sidual return for this portfolio of one stock and divides it by the residual standard deviation, the result is the information ratio (IR).

$$IR_P = \frac{Residual\ Return}{Residual\ Risk} = \frac{\alpha_P}{\omega_P}$$

Substituting the above information into the IR equation re-sults in an IR of .5. An IR of .5 is average when compared to other active portfolio managers according to Grinold and Kahn. The higher the IR the better the active strategy is at using information and turning it into positive alpha or residual return.

There are probably many financial advisors who are reading this book in an attempt to extract information that will help them with clients. For their sakes, assume all investors and clients are risk adverse. Assume meeting with a client and de-termining through proper consultation and the client's Invest-ment Policy Statement that the client has a tolerance for a portfolio with a residual standard deviation of 15%. The port-folio manager for this client should strive to build a portfolio with a residual standard deviation of 15% and classify this standard deviation as the optimal risk level and use this to de-termine the level of aversion to risk with the following formula:

$$\lambda_r = \frac{IR}{2 * \omega^*}$$

Where: IR = Information ratio
ω^* = Optimal level of Residual Risk
λ_r = Aversion to residual risk

Staying with the previous illustration, the portfolio manager's aversion to residual risk would be:

$$\lambda_r = \frac{.5}{2 * 0.15} = 1.667$$

Next, determine if the existing strategy adds value to the port-folio. The value-added equation from above is:

$$VA[P] = \alpha_P - \lambda_R * \omega_P^2$$

Insert inputs into the equation and receive a value-added of, 0.0333 or 3.33% (0.10 − 1.667 ∗ .04) of added return per year for the portfolio.

Before leaving the topic of residual returns and residual risk, it is important to bring attention to another similarity between MPT and quantitative active management, and that is to plot a frontier line with active parameters, residual return, and re-sidual risk. This frontier is similar to the total return to total risk efficient frontier because it too plots return versus risk. Since the benchmark has a residual return of zero, and the risk-free asset also has a residual return of zero, the frontier for active management begins at zero. This once again shows how active management and passive management are some-what linked in the aspects of quantitative analysis.

The Fundamental Law of Active Management [8]

The IR is a measure of a portfolio manager's opportunities. The Fundamental Law of Active Management described by Grinold and Kahn is an approximation to the IR and they use two attributes to approximate it. First is a strategy's breadth. They define breadth as the number of independent forecasts of exceptional return that are made in a given year. The next attribute is skill measured by a manager's information coeffi-cient, IC. The IC is described as the correlation of each forecast with the actual outcomes. It is easier to think of the IC as the manager's probability of success. The formula to approximate the IR is:

$$IR = IC * \sqrt{BR}$$

---

[8] Grinold & Kahn (1999)

Where:
IR is the Information Ratio
IC is the Information Coefficient
BR is the Breadth of the strategy.

Grinold and Kahn give a great example of applying the Fundamental Law of Active management and I will reproduce it here:

> "... Let us consider a gambling example. Since we want to be successful active managers, we will play the role of the casino. Let's take a roulette game where bettors choose either red or black. The roulette wheel has 18 red spots, 18 black spots, and 1 green spot. Each of the 37 spots has probability 1/37 of being selected at each turn of the wheel. The green spot is our advantage.
>
> If the bettor chooses black, the casino wins if the wheel stops on green or red. If the bettor chooses red, the casino wins if the wheel stops on green or black. Consider a \$1.00 bet. The casino puts up a matching \$1.00; that's the casino's investment. The casino will end up with \$2.00 (a plus 100 percent return) with probability 19/37, and with zero (a minus 100 percent return) with probability 18/37. The casino's expected percentage return per \$1.00 bet is
>
> $$\left(\frac{19}{37}\right) * (100\%) + \left(\frac{18}{37}\right) * (-100\%) = 2.7027\%$$
>
> The standard deviation of the return on that single bet is 99.9634%. If there is one bet of \$1.00 in a year, the information ratio for the casino will be 0.027038 = 2.7027/99.9634. In this case, our skill is 1/37 and our breadth is one.

The formula predicts an information ratio of 0.027027. That's pretty close.

We can see the dramatic effect breadth has by operating like a real casino and having 1 million bets of $1.00 in a year. Then the expected return will remain at 2.7027 percent, but the standard deviation drops to 0.09996 percent. This gives us an information ratio of 27.038. The formula predicts $(1/37) * \sqrt{1,000,000} = 27.027$.

The above example shows the simple notion that if a manager can swing the odds of success in his favor and do this over and over, he can be a successful portfolio manager. The difficulty with this simplified example is that it is difficult to know for certain that an investor has an edge on other participants in the market with any real degree of certainty and of course it is difficult to have the confidence to repeat the same strategy hundreds or as in the above example, a million times. As the above example shows, it does not take a vast amount of skill, only a slight advantage to create a positive information ratio, but it must be done repeatedly in order to increase the information ratio. A high IR is attainable in one of two ways based on the IR formula as mentioned above. Either the money manager has a high level of skill, a high level of breadth (which is how many times in a year he can repeat his successes), or a mixture of both. The fundamental law is merely a guide and should not be taken as fact and followed blindly.

As previously mentioned, the fundamental law of active management is simply a guiding theory that is extremely difficult to implement accurately since so many factors hinge on the manger's ability to be honest and true with themselves. As discussed earlier, investors are often overconfident and suffer from fundamental behavioral biases. This impedes their ability to distinguish fact from wishful thinking. One of the key assumptions of the theory is the portfolio manager must be able to accurately measure his ability and do so in an optimal way. This is extremely difficult to do but reveals that most managers may have great ideas and assumptions about financial markets; however, the key is the ability to turn these ideas into portfolios.

The next logical step is to combine what has been learned in order to build portfolios. To do this it is necessary to have an understanding that active management is nothing more than forecasting. The discussion on the CAPM provides a consensus forecast of expected returns if investors make rational decisions. Unfortunately it has yet to be proven empirically either for it or against it. Active managers must believe it is possible to construct portfolios that vary from a benchmark and believe in their ability to use information that varies from a benchmark in such a way as to, on average, provide exceptional returns.

First, it is important to find information that will lead to superior returns. This information can be drawn on from many sources, including the valuation chapters previously addressed. When using valuation methods, investors or managers are forecasting stock prices in hopes of using this information to add alpha to a portfolio. This unfortunately does not come with an instruction manual defining what information to use. If polled, 10,000 portfolio managers will probably offer 10,000 different ways to turn information into portfolios. Kahn and Grinold list several procedures to turn information into portfolios that range from building lists of buy, sell, and hold lists to quantitative approaches that require special technology. The most common technique for portfolio construction is the use of stock screens. Stock screens are the simplest method for organizing forecasted alpha on individual stocks. If the price to sales (P/S) ratio provides the information that can be used to forecast positive alpha, investors can build a screen that provides positive alpha. The next step is to de-termine a proper ranking methodology. For example, an in-vestor can screen the Dow Jones Industrial Average which is composed of 30 stocks and invest in the top ten stocks based on a subjective ranking method and sell short the bottom ten and rebalance or rescreen every week, every month, or every quar-ter. Screens are great for simplicity but have several downfalls as well. Depending on the investment universe size, it is pos-sible that a particular screen returns only stocks of a particu-lar sector which would cause an increase in risk exposure to that particular sector. Stratification is another way to build a portfolio. Stratification is using the results of a screen and or-ganizing or compartmentalizing the stocks. This is another at-tempt at diversifying a stock screen in an attempt to avoid dramatically overweighing any particular sector or industry. There are other methods of constructing a portfolio that go be-yond the scope of this book, such as quantitative methods us-ing linear regression as well as quadratic programming. As most investors are aware, portfolio construction is multifac-eted and can be accomplished in numerous ways. I wish I could tell a specific investor exactly how to build a portfolio that will produce a high information ratio consistently, but there is no sure way of doing this. If an investor is deeply committed to active portfolio management, I would definitely recommend Kahn and Grinold's Active Portfolio Management which pro-vides a remarkable technical appendix and will be a great ref-erence for years to come.

So far I have covered portfolio management using stock selec-tion as opposed to asset allocation. Some may be thinking there is no difference but there is. Asset allocation is often thought of as a passive investor's portfolio management con-cept, but actually it is an active management concept. In pas-sive portfolio management, strategic asset allocation is key where as active management relies on tactical asset allocation. Tactical asset allocation is the variation of asset allocation

around the strategic allocation mix in an attempt to outperform a benchmark and is a topic that will go beyond the scope
of this book. Interested individuals should study quantitative
methods in order to understand the full potential of regression
analysis.

An explanation of a few things will at least bring some clarity
to the concept. First tactical asset allocation involves time se-
ries regressions as opposed to cross sectional analysis, which
is a key difference between asset allocation and asset selection.
These time-series regressions are used to forecast which asset
class will likely outperform other asset classes. If considering
U.S. asset classes, an investor may look only at broad asset
classes such as cash, stocks, and bonds, or they may examine
a more detailed list of asset classes. I will summarize the process of active asset allocation, but as previously mentioned, linear regression models are outside the scope of this book.

This first step in asset allocation involves forecasting returns
on assets within a specific area. Assume an investor is only
interested in domestic equity and domestic bonds for allocating
portfolios. The first step is to run a regression using in-sample
data. Kahn and Grinold start half way through the in-sample
data in order to test the forecast's ability throughout the rest
of the in-sample time frame before moving on to out-of-sample
data. By doing this an investor can determine which coeffi-
cients are explaining returns more accurately. The next step
is to build optimal portfolios by using expected active returns
relative to an asset allocation benchmark as opposed to the
standard mean/variance optimal portfolio. The last step is to
test the model portfolio with out-of-sample data.

Another component of active portfolio management is benchmark timing. This is often a dubious task, and it is extremely
difficult to be a successful benchmark timer. Kahn and
Grinold define benchmark timing as an active management

decision to vary the managing portfolio's beta with respect to the benchmark. Kahn and Grinold use beta to define benchmark timing. They state that if a benchmark timer concludes the benchmark will do better than usual, the investor should increase beta above one. The same holds true for an expectation of a worse than expected benchmark return. In this case the beta should be reduced below one. Remember that benchmark timing is not asset allocation but merely speculation. If an investor used no other investing tool except the decision of either going long the equity markets or holding cash she may be able to address the difficulty of benchmark timing. When an investor thinks in terms of breadth at most benchmark timing can only give them a breadth of 365 if they forecast the direction of the market every day. Investors know from the IR equation that there are only two things that determine the IR and they are breadth and skill. Now if an investor knows breadth is low due the fact they are only forecasting one variable they are left with skill. Without any studies to back me up I would assume that forecasting the direction of the market on any given day likely has a 50/50 probability. Based on this knowledge alone, investors can conclude that while benchmark timing can add significant value, it is very difficult.

In order to implement an active strategy, investors must first turn raw data into useful information. Unfortunately this is up to the individual investor to develop. Remember the saying, "Garbage in, garbage out." Investors can attempt to link the important components necessary to develop an active strategy. First is the valuation methodology to forecast exceptional returns. This is central to active management. This is often difficult as investors must take raw information and turn it into portfolios. Assume for simplicities sake the use of a screen for valuation is used. Once a stock selection strategy has been developed, use the fundamental law of active management to determine the value the information brings to the table. Then move forward with the portfolio construction process.

Most investors do not attempt to maximize information ratios but attempt to make money; it is as simple as that. I would estimate that a majority will use valuation techniques and a fixed strategy for determining weights such as equally weighting all stocks within a portfolio as opposed to attempting to determine the appropriate weight to maximize alpha. It must be understood that active management is not a simple task and most definitely not for everyone. If hiring a professional money manager whether it is a third party money manager or a financial advisor who wants to charge a fee for active management, be sure to ask them this question. "Please explain to me your process for investing my money in such a way as to earn a positive information ratio?" If he or she gives a bologna answer, walk away and continue the search for a professional active manager.

Treynor/Black Portfolio Allocation Model

The Treynor/Black model for portfolio allocation is a combination of active and passive investing. The model, as mentioned, is an allocation model except instead of being a passive only or active only, the Treynor/Black (TB) model uses quantitative analysis to determine how much to allocate to the passive portfolio and how much to allocate to the active portfolio. This model was published in the "Journal of Business" in 1973 by Jack Treynor and Fischer Black. The TB model assumes investment markets are relatively efficient. I think most could agree that this is a rather feasible idea since market prices are in the news and information is disseminated very quickly; however, at times the pricing in of new information may not be correct and that eventually prices correct themselves toward a fundamentally intrinsic value. The TB model starts with a passive portfolio (P) which represents the market as a whole. The S&P 500 will be the proxy for the market for an example study of the TB model. TB also incorporates an active portfolio (A). Arriving at the active portfolio can be accomplished in a number of ways, but for the purposes of this book, assume valuation techniques are used.

The TB model tells us how much should be invested in the active portfolio and how much should be invested in the passive or market portfolio. The notation used in the previous section will be used here as well. I will be using residual return or alpha and residual variance to describe the active portfolio just as in the previous section.

Start with what TB refers to as the initial allocation to the active portfolio:

$$W_A^0 = \frac{\frac{\alpha_A}{\omega^2}}{\frac{r_b}{\sigma_b^2}}$$

Where:
W_A^0 = Initial Weighting of the Active Portfolio
α_A = Residual Return from the Active Portfolio or Alpha
ω^2 = Variance of Residual Return
r_b = Return on the Benchmark
σ_b^2 = Variance of Benchmark Return

This equation can be interpreted as saying if the numerator is high compared to the denominator, the total allocation to the active portfolio should increase, and if the denominator is high compared to the numerator, the total allocation to the passive portfolio should increase.

This equation holds true only if based on the assumption that the beta of the active portfolio is equal to one. Several institutional investors strive for a beta of one while reaching for positive alpha. But the beta on the active portfolio can vary from one significantly which would only alter the perception of the active portfolio.

Therefore the final weight of the active portfolio should take into consideration that beta can and often does differ from one. The TB equation for the final weight in the active portfolio is:

$$W_A^f = \frac{W_A^0}{W_A^0(1 - \beta_A) + 1}$$

This shows that the final active weight of the portfolio is proportional to the beginning weight and its beta. The investor now knows the final active weight, but what about the passive portfolio? The passive portfolio is equal to:

$$W_P^f = (1 - W_A^f)$$

Let us now look at a simplified example of how the TB model would work. Let us assume the following characteristics about the benchmark:

$r_b = 5\%$
$\sigma_b^2 = 225$ which equates to a 15% standard deviation

Let us use the oversimplified example from above:

Current Price: $20
Dividend: $1
Dividend Growth forever: 10%
Required Rate of Return (using CAPM): 15%

Recall the Gordon Constant Growth Rate model as:

$$V_0 = \frac{D_1}{r - g}$$

Using the above information there is a present value price of $22.

$$V_0 = \frac{1.10}{.15 - .10} = 22$$

The investor can conclude that the market is undervaluing this stock by $2 which is a forecasted residual return or alpha of 10%.

Assume that the standard deviation of residual return is 20%. This would imply that the expected price of $22 versus the market price of the stock over the time period moved up or down 20% versus its average.

These are the characteristics of our active and passive portfolio:

$\alpha_A = 10\%$
$\omega^2 = 400$
$r_b = 5\%$
$\sigma_b^2 = 100$ which equates to a 10% standard deviation
Using the equation for an initial weighting into the active portfolio would result in an allocation to the active portfolio of:

$$1.126 = \frac{\frac{10}{400}}{\frac{5}{225}}$$

This is equivalent to leveraging the active portfolio to 113% and shorting the passive portfolio 13%. This is essentially selling the passive portfolio in order to buy an additional 13% of the active portfolio. The allocation above would be the type of portfolio a hedge fund would love. However, there is one problem. Forecasts are prone to error and even a small error in the active residual return could ruin a leveraged portfolio. Assume the above portfolio is possible and a forecast beta of the active portfolio to be 0.8. How would this change the allocation among the active and passive portfolios?

The equation for the final weight to the active portfolio proves

$$W_A^f = \frac{W_A^0}{W_A^0(1 - \beta_A) + 1}$$

$$.919 = \frac{1.126}{1.126(1-.8) + 1}$$

This tells an investor that if the beta of the active portfolio were 0.8 instead of one investors would allocate 92% of an account to the active portfolio and 8% (1-.919) to the passive portfolio. Beta plays a critical role in this model. If the beta were two instead of zero, the active portfolio weight would have changed to nearly 150% and a short position in the passive portfolio of 50%. This is something that cannot be taken lightly. Forecasting beta or any parameter for that matter is extremely difficult and small variations in these assumptions can have drastic impact for portfolio managers.

The above example is over simplistic as most active portfolio strategies would probably consist of more than one stock or asset. If an investor believes multiple stocks are undervalued and will provide returns above market expectations, he or she can implement them into the TB model as well by using a few more basic formulas. So first determine the weight of each stock in the active portfolio. To do this, use the following equation:

$$W_i^0 = \frac{\alpha_i}{\omega_i^2}$$

Where:

W_i^0 = Initial weight of stock i based on residual return to residual variance

α_i = Alpha of stock i

ω_i^2 = Residual Variance of stock i

Once the "initial weight" of each individual stock is established, normalize these weights so that the weights are scaled to a value of one. This is simple and uses the following formula:

$$w_i = \frac{w_i^0}{\sum_{i=1}^{n} w_i^0}$$

This equation has scaled the weights so that they are equal to one. Now each of the securities in this active portfolio is weighted based on the amount of value each will bring to the portfolio. The more value per unit of risk the more weight to give them within an active portfolio. This is logical and reasonable in theory, but investors must be careful. Just as in all portfolio optimization models, small variance within any forecast can be disastrous to the portfolios. I again will address the fact that if an individual is unable to put in the time and do the homework on valuation, it would be unwise to implement a TB model. In the absence of knowledge, hire someone to help with this task or invest passively.

In a single stock scenario, the alpha for a stock determined from valuation is the alpha for the entire portfolio. To determine the alpha of a portfolio that is made up of multiple stocks use the following formula:

$$\alpha_A = \sum_{i=1}^{n} w_i \alpha_i$$

Where:
α_A= Alpha of the Active Portfolio
$\sum w_i \alpha_i$= Sum of the weight times alpha for each stock

The alpha for the active portfolio is composed of the alpha for each security multiplied by the weight it holds in the portfolio and each of these weighted alphas is summed up. If four securities with an estimated alpha of 3% each and a weight of 25%, the alpha of the portfolio would be 3%.

In addition to the alpha of the portfolio, it is necessary to know the residual variance of the active portfolio, ω_A^2. To arrive at the residual variation, use the equation:

$$\omega_A^2 = \sum_{i=1}^{n} w_i^2 \omega_i^2$$

The formula for the initial weight in the active portfolio is:

$$W_A^0 = \frac{\dfrac{\alpha_A}{\omega^2}}{\dfrac{r_b}{\sigma_b^2}}$$

Where:

W_A^0= Initial Weighting of the Active Portfolio
α_A= Residual Return from the Active Portfolio or Alpha
ω^2= Variance of Residual Return
r_b= Return on the Benchmark
σ_b^2= Variance of Benchmark Return

Please note that to obtain the initial weight of the passive portfolio an investor must subtract one from the initial weight of the active portfolio.

The initial weights make the assumption that the active port-folio has a beta of one. In reality this is not always true. To find the beta for the active portfolio, implement the following formula:

$$\beta_A = w_i \beta_i$$

Again this is a simple and easy equation for determining the beta of a portfolio. As demonstrated from the example on the single security portfolio, small errors in the beta estimate can cause drastic swings in the allocation between the active and passive portfolio. There are several other methods for deter-mining the appropriate betas for stocks other than the histor-ical method, and it is up to the individual to do additional homework to determine the method for forecasting and imple-menting financial models.

There is no difference in determining the final weights to the active and passive portfolio at this point. So for simplicity and ease of reference I have included the formulas below once again.

$$W_A^f = \frac{W_A^0}{W_A^0(1 - \beta_A) + 1}$$

$$W_P^f = 1 - W_A^f$$

Where:
W_P^f = The final weight allocated to the passive portfolio

It was the goal for this portion of the active management chap-ter to simplify as best as possible the TB model and active port-folio management as a whole. The models are fairly easy to understand on paper, but attempting to identify where the in-puts come from is rather challenging at times. Any seasoned professional money manager may find this text oversimplified and of little benefit, and that was the intention, to simplify the model in such a way that anyone willing to put in the time can understand the financial model without a background or advanced degree in finance.

Entire textbooks are filled with portfolio models and theories, and it is not my intention to list and identify all active portfolio strategies. I do however want to mention one final portfolio model, the Black-Litterman model. I will not go into great detail breaking down the formula in to bite size pieces as I did with the Treynor-Black model. Data on the Black-Litterman (BL) Model is accessible with very little effort, but it is worth mentioning here because it is one of the few financial models that is actually used in the real world.

The Black-Litterman Model is different from other portfolio management models because it allows portfolio managers to quantify forecasts that are quite complex which are called *views* and apply these views to portfolio construction. If an investor removes the portfolio manager's views and instead uses alpha forecast, the Black-Litterman model closely resembles the Treynor-Black model. The Black-Litterman model is best suited for asset allocation among broad asset classes such as foreign equity markets while the Trenor-Black model is best suited for individual stocks. Keeping with the objective of this book, I will not attempt to explain the intricacies of the Black-Litterman model. If an investor wants to investigate the BL model, it can be a great complement to the TB model. The BL model can be used for broad asset allocation decisions while the TB model can be used to deeply investigate those asset classes and provide an active portfolio allocation among individual stocks.

I must mention one final time that as with any financial theory or model, results are only as good as the inputs. Grinold and Kahn said it best, "Garbage in, Garbage out." Investors or portfolio managers will never find a model that is without flaws or errors in assumption. Some financial models are so complex that they are great in theory but fall apart in real world implementation. Can an analysis of the TB model clarify how to determine with certainty that the betas of each individual stock will not increase or decrease over our holding period? No. There is and will forever be an inherent risk in quantitative active management that the forecasts of the future might not materialize. I hope that after reading this chapter, it is clearer that there is more to portfolio management than being able to pick stocks. Success will depend on one of two things, luck or skill. Luck is luck because it must come to an end; skill on the other hand may go through periods of bad luck, but in the end will prevail.

Attempting to pick stocks in a mostly efficient market can be quite frustrating. It is difficult to outsmart the market in general. Even if markets are efficient, and investments are not able to provide a residual return, remember that there is still a place for portfolio management as a whole.

Up to this point, areas discussed have included valuation, passive management, and active management. Now it is time to move on to a more controversial topic within the investment community: Technical Analysis. The proper use of technical analysis used in conjunction with other forms of analysis such as the TB model provides opportunities for the active manager. It is when technical analysis is misused that it can be dangerous to the investor. The following section of this book will provide a basic knowledge of technical analysis and will let each individual decide if it can be beneficial to their portfolio management process.

[PART IV]

Technical Analysis

When hearing the words technical analysis, what comes to mind? Wouldn't it be great if an investor could use technical analysis to successfully predict stock prices. Some may think this concept is impossible and technical analysis is a waste of time and energy since most claim that stock prices move on a random walk, and it is therefore impossible to predict stock prices. A first attempt at understanding technical analysis may cause novice investors to wonder what this new idea is. Put as plainly as possible, technical analysis is a study of prices and price movement. A pure technical analyst does not need to read annual reports or study fundamentals. A technical analyst focuses time and energy on studying the price action of a company rather than studying the company itself. Recalling the study of market efficiency and the EMH, it is easy to come to the conclusion that a technical analyst is the biggest advocate for market efficiency. When a technical analyst studies a company, there exists a strong belief that all information that can and will cause a stock price to move is reflected in the current price. Stop and think about behavioral finance, and it is possible to come to the conclusion that the technical analyst also is an advocate for behavioral finance as well. Psychological factors such as fear and greed are impossible to predict but do influence stock prices. The pure technical analyst does not try to understand these issues and instead continues to study price action to determine the direction of the stock price based on the belief that these factors are already in the price. I however believe that technical analysis used in conjunction with fundamental analysis provides a better investment strategy than using either one in isolation.

Technical analysis is complex and just as everything in the world slowly evolves and changes to adapt to an ever changing environment, so too does technical analysis. I will attempt in the following chapters to give an overview of technical analysis (TA). This section of the book will be broke down into five chapters. First we will address the history of technical analysis to gain an understanding that this is by far not a new concept. The second chapter will break down technical analysis into is very broad components. We will study Dow Theory, trends, moving averages. The third chapter will focus on classic technical patters that have stood the test of time. We will move on to technical statistics in the fourth chapter as we look at relative strength, momentum and stochastics. We will then move on to the final chapter where we will discuss advanced technical techniques which will include Elliot wave analysis, Fibonacci, and Point and Figure charting. This part of the book will give you another tool for you investing tool kit.

[11]

Summarized History of Technical Analysis

E
ven though most technical analysts know technical analysis dates back hundreds of years, they still give credit to Charles Dow (1851-1902) for creating modern technical analysis. Charles Dow, as many know, is the creator of the Dow Jones Industrial Average which contains thirty large cap stocks. Dow created market indices in an attempt to represent the market as a whole and to predict which way the economy was heading. What some may not know is that Charles Dow is also the creator of Dow Theory which will be discussed later. What is more interesting is that investors often overlook how important a role Dow's company played in the development of technical analysis. Technical analysis is the study of price movement, but until Charles Dow started reporting each day's stock price quotes in his newsletter, which later become the Wall Street Journal, there was not a convenient way to record stock prices. As more people were able to see these stock quotes daily, more began studying these price movements in an attempt to predict stock prices. This was the beginning of technical analysis in the United States.

In the beginning all technicians plotted stock prices by hand. This at times could be labor intensive and hindered the analyst's ability to follow a large number of stocks. A handful of companies created charts and sold them to subscribers that were either too busy to chart them themselves or did not have the skill to do so accurately. With time came the dawn of the computer era. As early as the 1970's, computers began changing the landscape of modern technical analysis. Pioneers of technical analysis such as Robert Edwards and John Magee wrote books on chart patterns and pattern recognition that are as viable today as they were then. However, as the computers began to replace the hand drawn chart more complex technical calculations began to appear. If you were to google technical analysis techniques you would find an array of what have become known as technical indicators. Initially technical analysis was primarily pattern recognition. These are visual patterns that once drawn on a chart are identified by looking at the past price movement in an attempt to recognize patterns that are known to reoccur. The computer has given a more mathematical approach to the subject and hence the word "indicator." These indicators include such things as momentum and Moving Average Convergence Divergence (MACD), stochastics, and relative strength. These indicators could have been plotted by hand which would have required significant amounts of time.

Do not forget how competitive the stock market is and that technical analysis is not scientific. A chart pattern can be recognized, but an investor cannot be certain that the pattern will not fail. Later in the following chapters the discussion will focus on such things as whipsaws and why some indicators fail at times. It is important to think of technical analysis in the same context as stock valuation. This process is not to guarantee success but to increase the probability of success. As presented in the chapter on active portfolio management, an investor only needs to be right on average 51% of the time in order to be successful in active portfolio management. Technical analysis attempts to do just that: increase our probabilities of success. I believe John Magee says it best in his book Technical Analysis of Stock Trends (Edwards and Magee, 2009) when he said:

> When you enter the stock market, you are going into a competitive field in which your evaluations and opinions will be matched against some of the sharpest and toughest minds in the business. You are in a highly specialized industry in which there are many different sectors, all of which are under the intense study by men whose economic survival depends on their best judgement. You will certainly be exposed to advice, suggestions, and offers of help from all sides. Unless you are able to develop some market philosophy of your own, you will not be able to tell the good from the bad, the sound from the unsound.

[12]

Technical Analysis Basics

This is an advanced book on investing geared toward investment advisors and in some cases the more experienced do-it-yourselfer. However, I feel without at least a paragraph or two on the use of either bar charts or candlesticks will do the reader injustice. Chart construction using a computer is simple since the computer does all the heavy lifting. There are a couple of decisions that can have a rather dramatic impact on the overall experience with charting, and I would like to cover those differences here.

Candlestick charting versus bar charting. Candlesticks have been used in Japan for centuries but have only recently gained popularity in the U.S. The information used in Candlestick charts is the same as that of bar charts; they contain the high price for the time period used and the low price as well as the open and close for the day. An example of a Candlestick chart is below in Figure 12.01[9].

---

[9] All stock charts were built using Metastock Software.

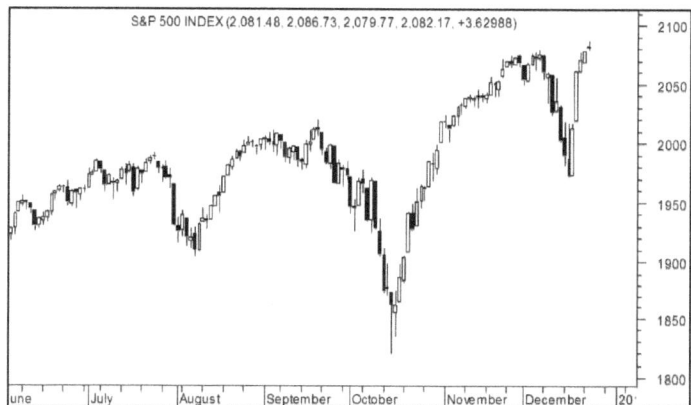

Figure 12.01

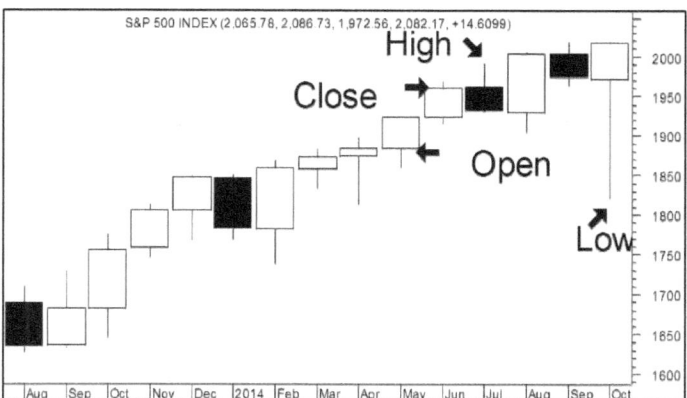

Figure 12.02

Figure 12.02 explains the candlestick information displayed on the chart: the high, low, open, and close. This is the system that I use for all my charts. Bar charts use the same information as candlesticks but display the price data differently. Figure 12.03 displays a typical bar chart.

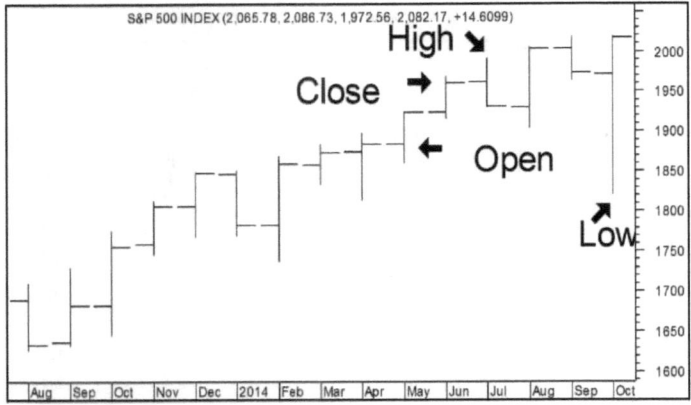

Figure 12.03

The above charts show the differences between the charting techniques. Candlesticks offer short-term patterns that have become increasingly popular with day traders and other short-term traders. I personally prefer candlestick charts because it is easier to see whether the price fell to the close or whether the price rose to the close. Deciding which way to display price data is an individual's decision. There are several other charting techniques and one of them in the chapter on advanced technical analysis is the Point and Figure.

Dow Theory

Charles H. Dow did not intend for his theory to be used as a guide in technical analysis but rather as a guide for economic conditions. Dow was not the one to bring Dow Theory to the mainstream; it was actually William P. Hamilton. Dow put forth his theory through a series of writings over 20 plus years. Hamilton organized Dow's principles to create the Dow Theory as it is known today.

Dow Theory is the best place for a beginner in technical analysis to begin. The most important concept in technical analysis is trend: is the trend up, down, sideways, changing course, and so on. It is easy to look at a chart and see that a trend is up or down. The most difficult part of technical analysis is identifying when a trend is changing. The closer an investor can get to the trend change, the more money that can be saved if the trend reverses down or the more money that can be made if the trend reverses up. Dow Theory is a study of general market trends. Dow noticed as did most people on Wall Street, that stocks tended to move together. In a bull market, most stocks went up, and in a bear market most stocks went down. There were the few cases where a stock would not follow the general market trend, but an intelligent investor would not base his investment decisions on stocks that tended to do so. These stocks would be nearly impossible to identify at the beginning of a trend change and would only be noticed through hindsight that they were one of the few that did not move with the general trend. Technical analysis is about increasing probabilities.

Based on Dow's knowledge regarding the general trend, he is believed to be the first to attempt to create an average price index in an attempt to determine the overall market trend. He created two Dow-Jones indices in January of 1897. One was composed of railroad companies which today include airlines and trucking companies, and the other was an index that represented the industrial companies. These averages have changed numerous times to keep them relevant to today's markets and economy.

Dow believed that the index averages discounted all information. He stressed that thousands of investors are economically tied to their abilities, so the markets include the best investors with the best information and therefore the markets discount everything. Does this sound familiar? Sounds like EMH doesn't it? An investor and student of Dow Theory must believe this and by doing so will be better able to understand the concept of trends.

Dow believed the market moved in three basic trends that were differentiated by time and depth. When thinking of bull and bear markets, most tend to think of prolonged movements in the same direction which would result in a trend. Dow called the prolonged movements the Primary Trend. Most of these trends tend to last from a year to several years only interrupted by what he called Secondary Trends. These Secondary Trends were in the opposite direction of the Primary trend. In a Primary trend, each rally after a secondary trend makes higher highs and each secondary trend makes a higher low. Figure 12.1 gives an example of a Primary trend and the many secondary trends that interrupt the primary trend. As indicated in the chart, each secondary wave did not go lower than the one before it, and each secondary moved higher than the last high. These secondary reactions make up the primary trend. The third type of trend Dow mentions is the minor trends. These trends tend to last only a few days and the average investor should not be concerned as these moves are largely noise. Only the short-term trader should be concerned with the minor moves of the market. Dow believed that the true investors should be concerned only with the Primary trend. The goal of the investor is to identify as soon as possible the change in primary tend and to enter positions as early as possible in a bull trend and sell as quickly as possible in a bear trend or possibly go short. Primary trends have three phases. The first is usually when media and corporate outlooks are still dim, but investors are seeing signs that in the months ahead that the economy and market should be doing better, and therefore place their investments at this early stage, and the markets begin to change. This is the phase Magee and Edwards call the *accumulation phase*. At this early stage, earnings reports and media attention are often at their worst. As corporate earnings begin showing signs of improvement and the overall economy begins to improve, things move into the second phase of the primary bull market. This is when most traders are able to identify the trend and increase profits by entering this part of the primary trend as early as they can. As the public begins to take notice of the surging markets, investors begin to pile into the markets. Corporate earnings are at their best, and the media is touting how strong the bull market is. This is the bubbling phase as most people have forgotten about the previous primary bear and focus only on the present. This is the stage when the market is generally asking what to buy, and the institutions are asking what to sell.

A Primary bear market is similar to the primary bull except it deals with the emotions of fear instead of greed. Magee and Edwards call the first phase of a primary bear the *distribution* phase. This is when the smart money is asking what to sell in the latter phase of the previous primary bull market. As advisors and investors know, the market tends to fall faster than it rises. So the second phase of a primary bear market is when the public begins to panic and sell no matter the news. The last phase of a primary bear market is when there are no buyers in the market. This is the phase when the media is reporting the worst case scenarios and corporate profits are at their worst. Toward the end of this primary bear, the tide changes and the first phase of a primary bull begins. This happens over and over and over and the only thing not known for certain is how long each phase will last and when each begins and ends. This information is of course only available through hindsight, and as indicated in the study of biases, hindsight is a killer to investor's returns.

Figure 12.1

Secondary trends are also important. As previously mentioned, secondary trends are the pullbacks during bull markets and the rallies during bear markets. Figure 12.1 shows secondary trends within the larger bull market. The importance is in the retracement of the previous intermediate price move in the primary direction. There can and often are several secondary corrections during the duration of a primary move.

Figure 12.2

Figure 12.2 shows a secondary reaction and its retracement. Most secondary reactions will retrace anywhere from one-third to two-thirds of the previous move in the primary direction.

The above chart shows that the secondary reaction retraced about two-thirds of the swing in the primary direction. This is not a hard and fast rule but rather a guide to trend analysis. The Secondary corrective move is where most investors stall. Most of the time these corrective moves can be misleading and are not as obvious as the one shown above in the chart. These corrective moves are further explained in the advanced techniques chapter with a discussion of Elliot Wave analysis and Fibonacci analysis.

The minor trends should be considered noise by the average investor. These are the minor fluctuations of the day to day movement of the market and make up the intermediate trends. Dow considered the minor moves to be meaningless to the average investor and completely unreliable in identifying trends. In Dow's time, day traders were almost nonexistent unless they owned a seat on the floor of the stock exchange. The advent of the computer, day trading, and the growing numbers of investors trading in very short time periods would have likely astonished Dow.

Indices Must Confirm

The two index averages Dow created are the Transportation average and the Industrial average. Dow used these two indexes to determine a primary trend change. A confirmation occurs when both averages reach new highs or new lows. The chart below contains both the Dow Jones Industrial Average and the Dow Jones Transportation Average. The chart shows that when the Transportation average on the bottom made a new high, it was not confirmed by the Industrial Average. Robert Rhea stated, "Conclusions based upon the movement of one average, unconfirmed by the other, are almost certain to prove misleading." This would have most certainly been the case for Figure 12.3. The confirmation among the averages need not occur on the same day; however, the trends are not considered valid unless they confirm each other. One can make a high one day and the other can make a high a day, a week, or a month later, and the trend should not be acted upon until the trend is confirmed by both averages.

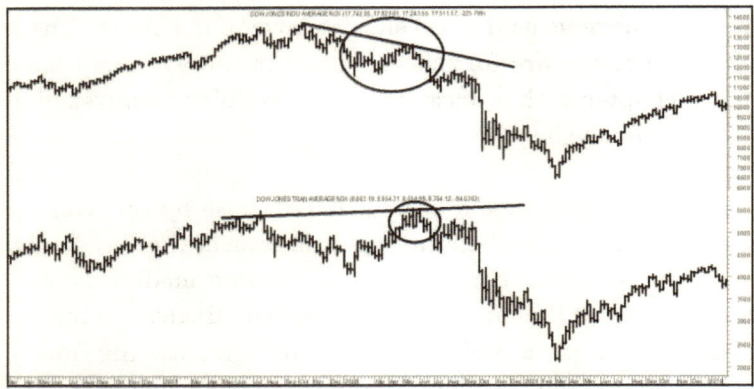

Figure 12.3

Kirkpatrick and Dahlquist (2011) state,

> Confirmation, therefore, is the necessary means for recognizing in what direction the primary trend is headed. Failure to reach new levels during a secondary reaction is a warning that the primary trend may be reversing. For example, when there is a primary bull market, the failure of the averages to reach new highs during a secondary advance alerts the analyst that the primary trend may be reversing to a bear market. In addition, if lower levels are reached during the secondary bear trend, it is an indication that the primary trend has changed from an upward bull trend to a downward bear trend.

Investors and account managers must understand that the economy of the 1900s was quite different from our serviced based economy of the 1990s and 2000s. When Dow created Dow Theory, the United States was primarily a manufacturing economy. It is easy to see the railroads which made up the transportation index and industrials were highly correlated. If the industrials shipped less product, it was reasonable to assume that the railroads would suffer since they were losing business, and if the railroad's earnings began to suffer, investors could infer that industrials may not be manufacturing as much product. Today, in contrast with the early 1900s, the U.S. is primarily a serviced based country, so a different approach is necessary for trend confirmation. Kirkpatrick and Dahlquist have proposed using the S&P 500 index and the Russell 2000 index as the S&P 500 index represents the largest companies in the U.S. and the Russell 2000 index represents smaller more technologically based companies. When the two indexes confirm, the primary trend is confirmed.

The major criticism of Dow Theory is that it is often late to the party. By the time the second leg down after the first secondary reaction makes a lower low, the market is often well off its previous highs. Dow would argue that if investors failed to wait for the primary trend reversal and confirmation they would trade too often and be whipsawed so much that it would pay to wait a little longer before giving up on a trend.

Reversal Patterns and Trends

Dow has shown that identifying a trend gives the investor the highest probability of success. So how do investors identify primary trends or any trend for that matter? Trends are extremely easy to identify… in hindsight. Any investment advisor who claims to be a technician will likely claim he or she uses some form of trend analysis. The reason for this is that trends are easy to identify on a chart. Look at the Figure 12.4 below.

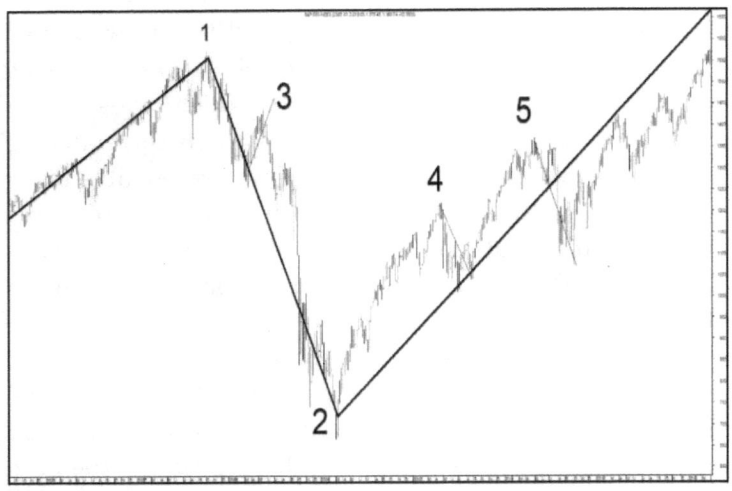

Figure 12.4

From the far left side of the chart, it is easy to see that the trend was up until it reached point 1. It is also easy to see the trend from point 1 to point 2. Refer to the chapter on behavioral biases and reread hindsight bias, and it is obvious why this chart is deceptive. I want to point out something that I believe is the most important thing to remember when studying technical analysis. It is impossible to predict what will happen next on the far right hand side of the chart. What I want an investor to do is study this chart and write down why to sell point 1, or better yet where to sell after point 1. What is the difference between the pattern at point 1 and the pattern at points 3, 4, and 5? Looking at the chart it is easy to see where the trend started and where the trend ended. What is difficult is doing the exact same thing but not knowing the right side of the chart. Will the trend continue or has it reversed? For example, look at the eight charts below. After reviewing each chart make a determination as to whether the primary trend continues or whether it has reversed. Each successive chart is moving forward in time so this is an attempt to prove a point regarding the difficulty of identifying when a primary trend has reversed. Here we go.

Figure 12.5

Will this trend continue?

Figure 12.6

Has the trend reversed?

Figure 12.7

It looks as though that was a secondary reaction to the primary trend.

Figure 12.8

What about now? I am still moving though time with each chart.

Figure 12.9

Secondary reaction or trend change?

Figure 12.10

Secondary reaction or Trend change?

Figure 12.11

It looks as though that was a definite trend change from a Primary Bull to a Primary Bear. The question is where to sell or if to sell? Last chart. Secondary reaction or trend change?

Figure 12.12

Another reversal and trend change. My hope is that through this exercise it is easier to understand that the key to successfully applying technical trend analysis is to identify a trend as early as possible and to cut mistakes before they carry on for too long. If an investor had thought that one of the secondary trends in an earlier chart was an actual trend reversal and sold or sold short, it would have been a mistake. Investors must recognize a mistake even better than an actual change in trend. Learning from mistakes can be costly.

In this section I hope to help provide a better understanding of the structure of trends and how best to identify them. As the chart study demonstrated, making money on trend analysis seems easy in concept but is difficult in practice. What many advisors and individual investors find difficult about technical analysis is its subjectivity. I will never be able to tell a client that there is a hard and fast rule to identify a trend reversal. This is what makes technical analysis an art form just as much as rules based. Many technical analysts find it mandatory to create trading rules. As stressed in the behavioral chapter, I recommend to all the advisors and investors to start a trade journal. This will help identify weaknesses in the investor's mind and personality and help identify mistakes and eliminate repeated mistakes. Einstein said it best, "Insanity is doing the same thing over and over expecting different results." Keep a trade journal and avoid insanity.

An investor can profit first from identifying trends as early as possible and riding the trend until it completes. The second advantage is identifying when the trend has run its course and exiting the positions as early as possible after the trend has reversed. The key to remember is "after the trend has reversed," not before. A new trend is normally identified after a previous trend is broken in the opposite direction. Reversal patterns often can be spotted before the previous trend is broken and once the trend is broken it should be acted upon. A previous trend must be broken before a new trend can begin; it is that simple. It is simple until investors are distracted by the noise of financial markets. Often times a trend line will be broken in the opposite direction of the prevailing trend only to reverse back to the same direction. The best way to learn technical analysis is to teach it in a way that advisors and clients are put in as real a situation as possible. The following pages advance through a time series of the same chart in an attempt to show what it is like trying to identify trends and their reversals. The previous charts showed that trend changes can often be confused with secondary reactions, and often times the trend has changed long before investors would react. Now look at how to properly construct a trend line and walk through another time-series of charts to provide clarity.

A trend-line is nothing more than connecting peaks and troughs. Connecting these peaks and troughs make it possible to determine the trend of the market. Figure 12.13 is an example of an uptrend line constructed by connecting the low trough points. This line that connects the trough points is called **Support.**

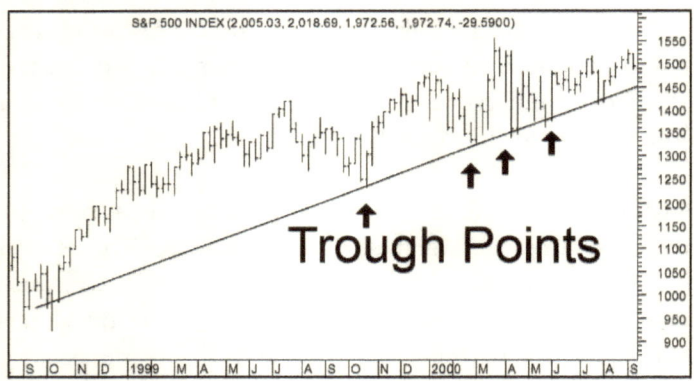

Figure 12.13

Figure 12.14 is an example of a downtrend constructed by connecting the peak points. The line connecting the peak points is called **Resistance.**

Figure 12.14

Determining when to sell or buy is based on whether the trend line is broken to the up side or down side. If the prevailing trend is down and a trend line can be drawn by connecting the peak points, an advisor or investor should sell when the price breaks above the trend line identified by connecting the peak points as in Figure 12.15 below.

Figure 12.15

The next chart, Figure 12.16 is a downside breakout as the price falls through the upward sloping trend line.

Figure 12.16

This is the most basic form of trend analysis, but with simplicity comes the increased probability of error. Look through a
time-series of charts to get a better understanding of the com-
plexity that surrounds such simplicity. Does Figure 12.17 below would indicate that there was a previous up trend that has
been violated and a new down trend has begun?

Figure 12.17

It is obvious that the previous down trend-line has been broken
to the upside. Has the trend reversed?

Figure 12.18

Following the most basic trend rules supports the position that the trend line is broken to the upside as in the Figure 12.18 above. However, as shown in Figure 12.19, simplicity can often lead to confusion which leads to frustration and mistakes.

Figure 12.19

The trend line is broken to the upside but fails, and the price continues to fall. This is most certainly frustrating, and an experienced technician is able to recognize the mistake and cut losses early. The same chart is shown below in Figure 12.20

and gives an example of how to cut losses. If a trend line breaks out, investors can do a couple of things: wait for confirmation which requires patience and additional rules or use any secondary reaction as the first trough and if the price falls below this level, cut losses.

Figure 12.20

Another element to keep in mind when drawing a trend line is it must be drawn correctly or not drawn at all. If a trend line touches only one point or does not touch any points, meaning has been afforded to something that is absolutely meaningless. So it is paramount to draw trend lines correctly. What I like to do is start by connecting the first and second peak or trough and extend the line without moving it up or down. This allows a view of a trend line without manipulating it. Beginners often have difficulty with this because they tend to want make the charts agree with assumptions. Again, look back at the behavioral biases chapter and note that confirmatory bias is the behavior described. It is paramount to analyze charts with as little bias as possible and this starts by knowing the basics.

At times it is necessary to adjust the trend lines. If an investor trades momentum securities, he or she may be frustrated by following trend lines alone. Look at the following example of a trend line that is broken because of a change in momentum.

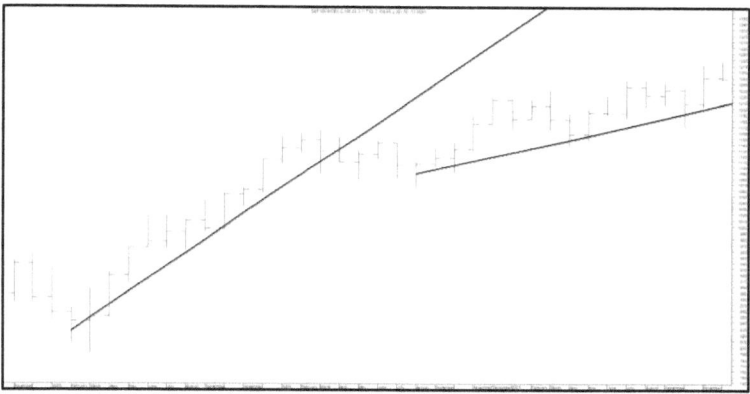

Figure 12.21

In Figure 12.21 the first trend line is strong and proceeds for quite some time, but the security changes gears and continues in the primary trend with less momentum than before. There are only three things that can happen when a trend line is violated. The obvious is there is a trend reversal, but the less obvious is when a trend line is broken and the stock is simply on a secondary reaction and consolidates, and the third is when a security either slows in momentum or increases momentum. Adding a trend line to the top of an uptrend trend line and to the bottom of a downtrend trend line yields a channel. Channels are useful for several reasons. First they provide an area of support and resistance as a guide for the direction of the market. If during an uptrend, the price breaks out above the top resistance line, this could mean the stock is gaining momentum or could mean this is the beginning of a reversal.

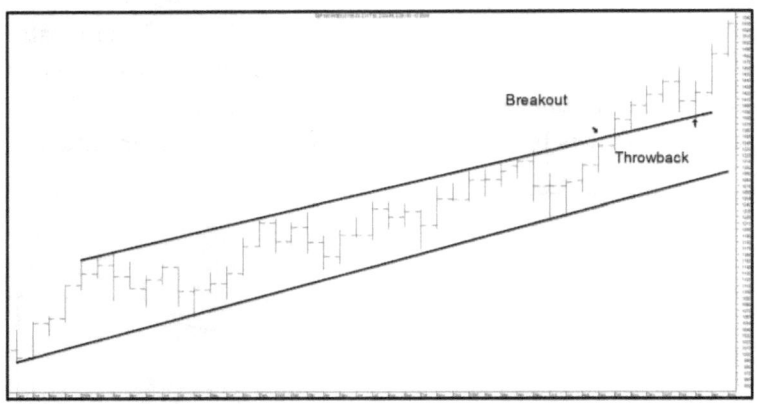

Figure 12.22

Figure 12.22 shows a change in momentum. This chart indi-cates that if the line had been drawn on the lower trend line it is possible to have missed the new trend line which is being formed where the security has what is called a throwback which is another way of saying a secondary reaction after a breakout. If investors entered a position at the breakout point in Figure 12.22, they would watch carefully for the throwback making certain it did not penetrate the upper trend line. Once the throwback has occurred and it has bounced off the upper trend line, it is advisable to take a position if an investor has not already done so and enter at this juncture or add to the position entered earlier at the initial breakout. The upper trend line is now supported since the security has obviously gained momentum.

There are also rules that some technical analysts apply to trend lines and breakouts. Robert Edwards and John Magee in their classic book titled *Technical Analysis of Stock Trends,* state that a breakout should not be classified a true breakout unless it breaks out by more than 3%. They state that this is not a hard and fast rule but like all technical analysis is a mere guideline and one should be cautious of a breakout that does not attain 3% before a throwback occurs. If there is a breakout, but it is not able to stay above the upper trend line, an exhaustion breakout has occurred which means it was a false breakout and if acted upon should be sold immediately. As investors gain experience they will notice that false breakouts are common and it is desirable to get a feel for the stocks movement and analyze past price movement to see whether false breakouts are common for that particular stock.

Volume

The most cited confirmation statistic is volume. Volume is the psychological barometer of the stock market. Volume is usually measured daily but can be measured using other time frames. Volume is a great indicator that is not directly correlated to price. This helps avoid multicollinearity, which is where the correlations among independent variables such as stochastics and relative strength are strong. Volume can be used with any technical indicator and avoid multicollinearity. However, volume in my opinion is misleading. Most technical analysis literature states that rising price should be accompanied by rising volume and that volume leads price and so forth. In my own studies, I have found this is not the case. I have found that volume tends to spike during market sell offs and begins to taper off on the following market rally. Figure 11.23 is an example.

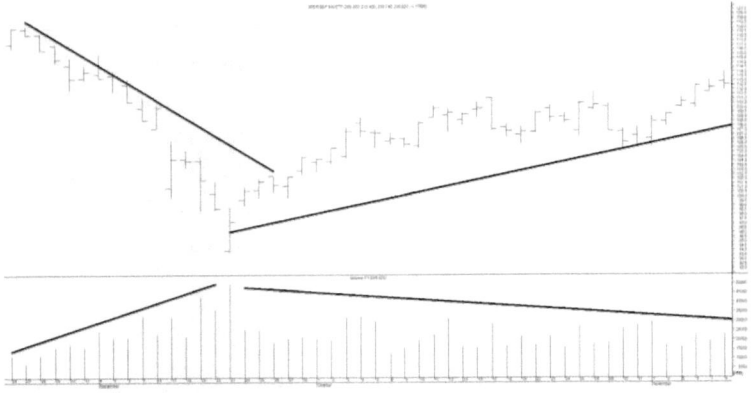

Figure 12.23

As demonstrated, when the market capitulated to the down-side, volume increased to its highest level. As the trend re-versed, a technical analyst waiting for confirmation on volume never sees it in Figure 12.23. Figure 12.24 below shows vol-ume over a six year period. Each spike in volume corresponds with a low in the security, not a high. Does this mean the other writers are wrong? Absolutely not. This book is about invest-ing not trading. There is a difference, and I will not attempt to explain it here. What I will say is that trading is generally focused on the short-term. Volume in the short-term appears to be more accurate than volume in the intermediate and longer-term. In the longer-term, use volume only at the begin-ning of trend to confirm a reversal, but in my experience vol-ume provides little accuracy for trend analysis.

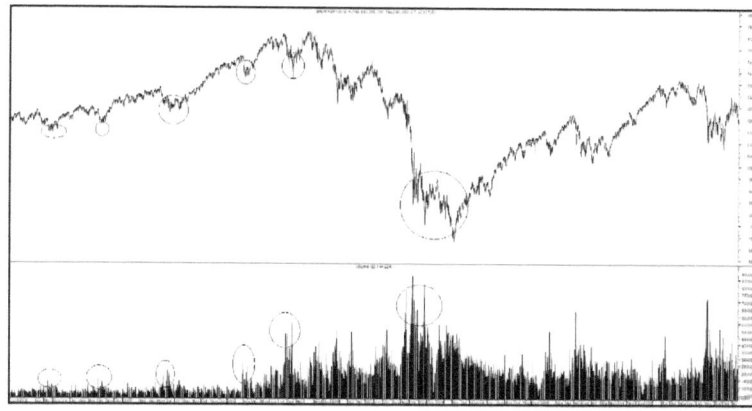

Figure 12.24

Some writers would look at Figure 12.25 and claim that there is a rise in volume until the peak in the market as shown in Figure 12.25. However, the increase in volume corresponds with each successive selloff and not with each new high. As stated, volume can be a great confirmation indicator and we will readdress it when we discuss price patterns.

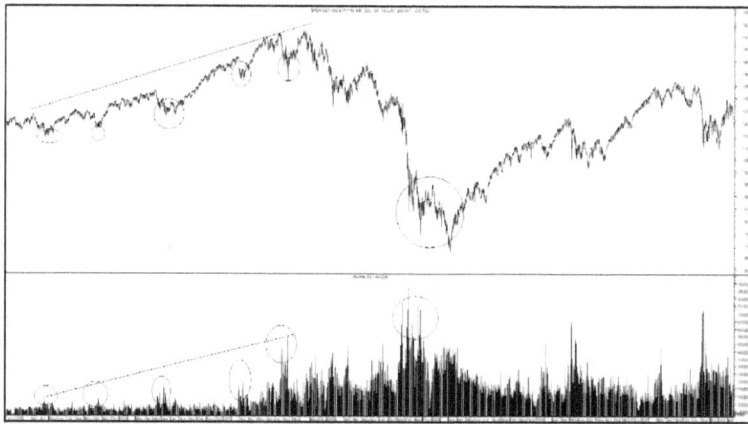

Figure 12.25

Moving Averages

The moving average in technical analysis is another basic tool but effective. When investors look at charts they are inun-dated with the choppiness of the markets. At times this chop-piness does nothing but confuse the technician and create an environment of indecisiveness. A moving average smooths out the daily volatility and allows the analyst to focus on the trend instead. The concept of moving averages is very simple, and the length of the moving average will determine the time hori-zon the analyst is interested in.

There are several different styles of moving averages. The most basic is the Simple Moving Average (SMA) which is the arithmetic moving average. To calculate a 10-day/period SMA, take the latest ten days, add up the prices, and divide by ten. Most computer charting software calculates the moving aver-age, so there is no need to focus much attention on the calcula-tion but instead on the interpretation.

The shorter the periods the "faster" the moving average reacts to price changes. The 10-day SMA would react more quickly to a price swing than the 50-day SMA. Figure 12.26 provides an example of the 10-day SMA and the 50-day SMA. As shown the 10-day reacts quicker to price movements in either direc-tion than does the 50-day.

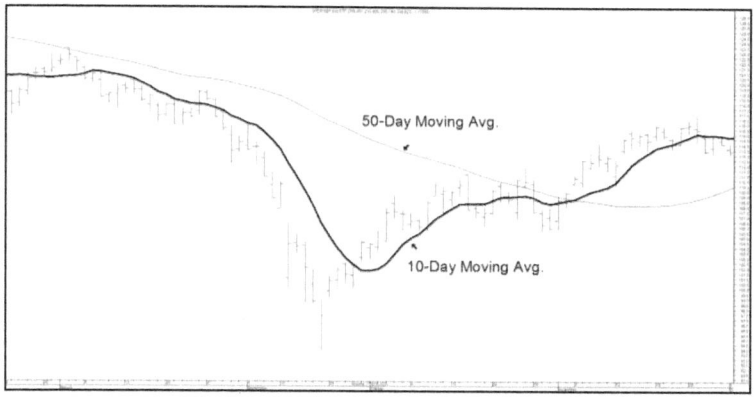

Figure 12.26

The most basic method for using the SMA to determine when to buy and sell a security is to buy when the price moves up through the moving average and to sell when the price moves below the moving average. Figure 12.27 illustrates this point using a 50-day SMA.

Figure 12.27

The longer the time period, the more data observations are included. This can be a blessing and curse. The blessing is that investors will react more slowly to small secondary reactions in the market; the curse is the reaction will be slower to a trend reversal. Figure 12.28 shows a 10-day SMA in place of the 50-day in Figure 12.27. The 50-day SMA would have kept an investor from buying and selling multiple times during a sideways market which is known as being whipsawed. At the same time, the investor would have entered later on the latest buy signal. Both have advantages and disadvantages, and an investor should match an SMA strategy to an overall investment horizon.

Figure 12.28

Which moving average timeframe is best for this SMA strategy? I hate to be the bearer of bad news but there is not a "best" SMA time frame. It must be taken as fact that no matter the time period, the SMA strategy will suffer whipsaws from time to time and will either be early or late depending on the timeframe, but even with these drawbacks, the moving average is a vital tool for all technical analysts.

The Exponential Moving Average (EMA) is identical to the SMA except the most recent price data is weighted heavier than the older price data. In the SMA calculation, all price data are equally weighted, so in a 10-day moving average, the price ten days ago has the same influence as the price that occurred yesterday. Some technicians believe yesterday's price should hold more weight than older prices and therefore prefer the EMA to the SMA. I will not go into how to calculate the EMA here since most charting software will calculate and plot the EMA. To learn more about the EMA calculation, read an article I published in the February 2012 issue of *Technical Analysis of Stocks and Commodities,* titled *Trading Momentum.* It is critical to remember that the EMA will react quicker to price changes than the SMA plotted using the same timeframe. Figure 12.29 compares the 50-day EMA and the 50-day SMA.

Figure 12.29

The thick line is the 50-day SMA, and the thin line is the 50-day EMA. Notice the EMA is quicker to respond to a price move than the SMA, and because of this investors have the same issue as presented with the shorter moving average versus the longer moving average, one responds quicker but could result in more whipsaws, and one responds slower and could delay identifying a trend change.

Moving Average Crossover

The Moving Average Crossover (MAC) is a common technical signal that is often quoted in the media. The MAC over works by taking a faster moving average and plotting it with a slower moving average. The most popular crossover parameters is the 50-day SMA plotted with the 200-day SMA. When the 50-day crosses below the 200-day SMA, it is called the death cross, and when the opposite occurs, it is commonly referred to as the golden cross. Figure 12.30 charts the 50-day SMA versus the 200-day SMA.

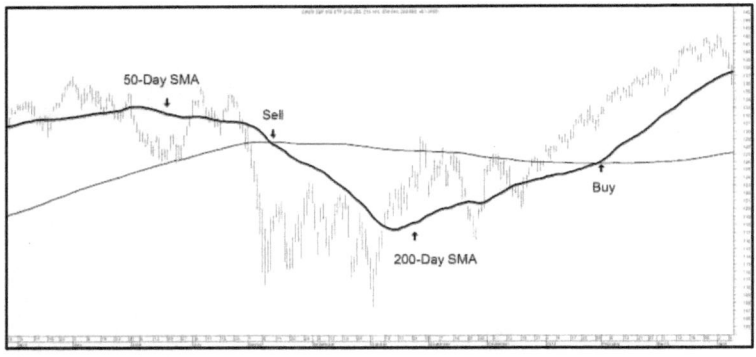

Figure 12.30

Look at the left side of the chart where the 50-day first crosses the 200-day SMA. This is obviously not the ideal time to sell this particular security; in fact it is the worst possible time. If an investor were holding this security and sold at this first signal and bought back at the next buy signal, he or she would have suffered a pretty severe whipsaw. This particular indicator is touted in the media anytime it occurs in the broad stock market indices. The only time such as long-term indicator is profitable is during prolonged moves whether it is a prolonged bull or bear market. To increase the sensitivity of the MAC strategy, it is necessary to decrease both the long and short-term moving averages.

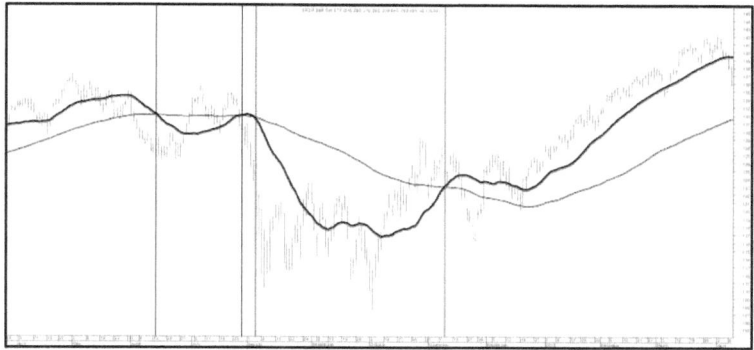

Figure 12.31

Figure 12.31 shows a 25-day SMA represented by the thick line and a 100-day SMA represented by the thin line. Each of the vertical lines represent the buy and sell signals generated by this crossover strategy. Look back at Figure 12.30 which is the same chart and notice the difference in the number and timing of the trades between these two strategies. This is why it is critical for a technical analyst to choose indicators and associated timeframes wisely.

The crossover strategy holds true for all styles of moving averages. Moving averages can also be used on weekly charts. Remember, when using a 10-day moving average and switching to a weekly chart, the charting software will automatically switch the moving average to a weekly periodicity. There are several different styles of moving averages, but I find all typically provide similar signals. Moving averages are best utilized as trend confirmation indicators as opposed to actual buy and sell indicators. If an investor has a correctly plotted trend line for example and it is broken in the opposite direction of the trend while simultaneously an MAC has occurred, use this as the confirmation of the trend break. In Figure 12.32 below it can be seen that the MAC occurred at nearly the exact same time that the down trend was broken to the upside. This would have given a clear confirmation that the trend has reversed,

and a position should be taken. Notice that most of the time
an investor will not be blessed with such clear cut decisions,
and as the time horizon decreases, it becomes fuzzier. If this
is an investor's first attempt at technical analysis, I recommend using longer term indicators. Beginning technical analysis is like being nearsighted and trying to look across the
street without glasses: everything is fuzzy and clouded. As investors gain experience and begin keeping a trade journal,
they will notice that charts begin to come into focus. It is at
this point an investor should begin to shorten their time horizon and focus on intermediate term trends. Attempting to
jump in head first right from the start will cause frustration
and the losses will increase.

Figure 12.32

[13]

Classic Technical Patterns

In the previous chapter I discussed the fundamentals of technical analysis which included trend lines. In this chapter on classic patterns, it will become clear that trend lines play an important role in price pattern recognition. There are only two main types of price patterns, reversal and continuation/consolidation patterns. Most advisors that I mentor seem to focus solely on reversal patterns thinking they want to be able get in or out of investments before it is too late. In studying these reversal patterns, I often find flawed knowledge regarding when a pattern should be acted upon and when it should be ignored. I will attempt to address that in this section.

I will start with reversal patterns since of course these are the most popular. The most hyped reversal price pattern is the head and shoulder pattern (HS). It is the most talked about and the most misunderstood of all reversal patterns.

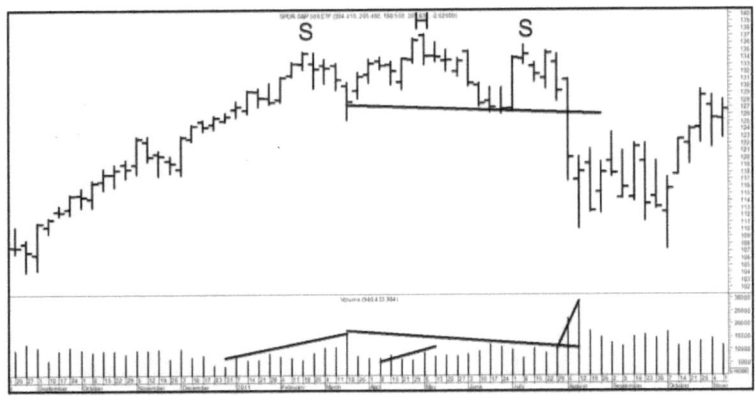

Figure 13.32

Figure 13.32 is a classic example of a Head & Shoulder pattern. If used correctly this is the most reliable reversal pattern
used. The key is understanding the psychology behind this indicator. The head and shoulder pattern gets its name from the
shape of the pattern itself. A strong rally will generally pre-
cede the left shoulder labeled "S." Investors never know that
a left shoulder has developed until they are able to make out
the other two components of the pattern. This is where an investor should take notice of volume. Volume will likely rise
toward the end of the left shoulder with lower volume during
the secondary pullback. As the market rallies to new highs,
notice that there is less volume than there was on the left
shoulder. From "H" in the above head and shoulder pattern,
see another sell off that should stop in the same area as the
preceding secondary. Another rally does not make new highs
and falls in the same vicinity as the previous shoulder. This
last rally will probably be on the weakest volume of the entire
pattern. What tends to happen to most investors when they
see this pattern is that they anticipate the move down. That
is a grave mistake when analyzing this pattern because it can
just as easily bounce off the neckline support and continue
with the previous trend. Many investors know this is a reversal pattern, but most do not realize that it is only a reversal

pattern if all criteria are met. To confirm this is a true head and shoulder pattern, the price needs to fall below the neckline after the right shoulder. Edwards and Mcgee recommend their standard 3% rule for this pattern as well. The price should fall below the neckline by 3% before this is a confirmed HS pattern. Notice in the above chart that the neckline is nothing more than a support line that is running sideways.

Volume in this pattern is important as it is in all the patterns studied here. The key to volume is knowing that it does not have to occur in order for the pattern to be valid. The best way to look at volume especially volume relating to reversal patterns is that volume does not have to occur but it increases the probability of success. If volume is not present, do not disregard the entire pattern, rather monitor it closely and remain cautious. Remember as a technical analyst, expertise will come with experience. Suppose an investor spots a head and shoulder pattern. It meets all criteria, breaks the neckline with significant volume and yet prices reverse and continue to move higher. This is rare and in most cases the error is on the side of the investor either losing patience or falsely identifying the pattern.

The head and shoulders pattern can also help a technician anticipate the approximate price level after the pattern has been confirmed.

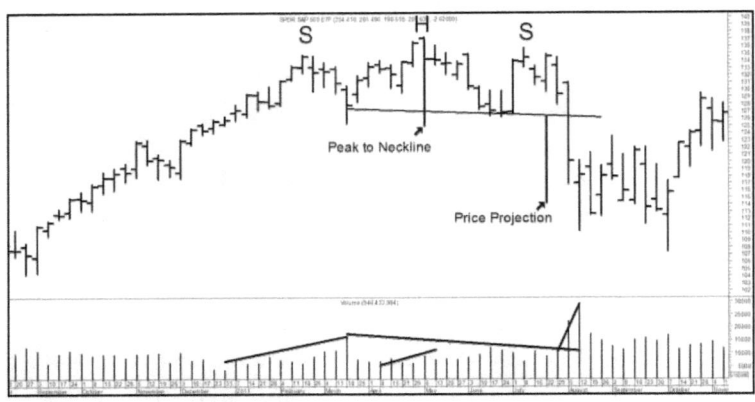

Figure 13.33

Figure 13.33 shows how to use the pattern to predict an approximate price target. Take the distance from the peak of the head to the neckline, confirm the pattern and then start at the neckline and measure lower, this will give the approximate distance the price could fall once the neckline is pierced as indicated by the thick black marks in Figure 13.33.

An inverse head and shoulder pattern can occur when a primary bear trend is reversing. Figure 13.34 is an example of an inverse head and shoulders pattern. Notice that the neckline is sloping upward and the right shoulder did not fall to the left shoulder's low. This is completely normal as most head and shoulder patterns do not look perfect. The same rules that applied to the regular head and shoulder pattern apply here.

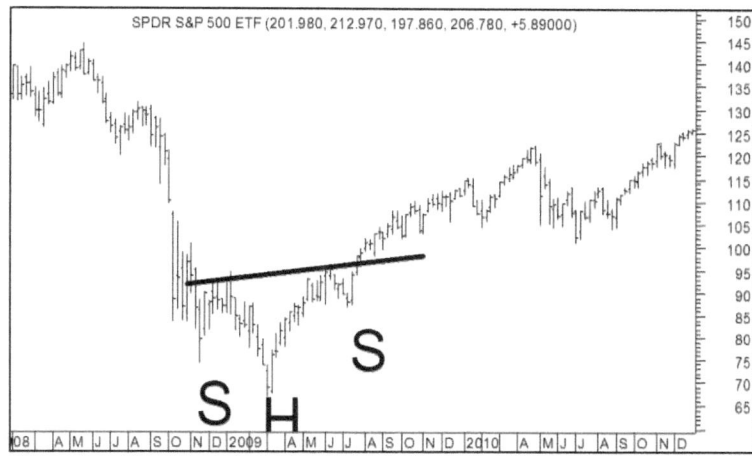

Figure 13.34

Rounding Top and Bottom

Studying reversal patterns will reveal that most trends take considerable time to reverse. The entire psychology of the market must change. Think of it like this, a consumer goes into a store with a particular item, and a store salesman attempts to change the shopper's mind. Will the prospective consumer change to this new idea or item? No. most stop, think about it, and make a purchase. This is the same process for the investment markets. As new information is being "sold" to the market, the market must digest this new information and determine whether its weight is enough to cause an entire change in the future outlook. There are times in extreme situations when the markets turn on a dime, but a majority of the time they are slow and well thought out directional changes that can be identified with reversal patterns. In order to be successful in identifying reversal patterns, be patient. When behavioral biases flare up during market volatility, be patient and wait for confirmation. This will take an enormous amount of focus and will be extremely difficult for the beginner.

The Rounding Bottom is actually a variation of the head and shoulders pattern because it eases the transition with no real identifiable head or shoulders, hence the name. The most popular rounding bottom pattern is known as the "Cup with Handle." This is the most popular because William O'Neil, founder of Investor's Business Daily, has built an entire trading concept around this pattern.

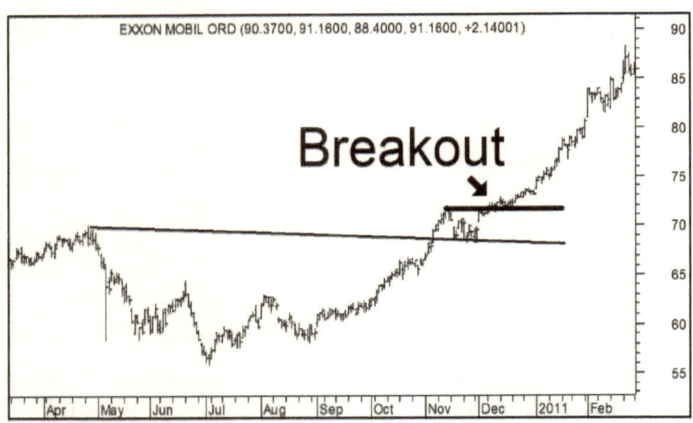

Figure 13.35

Figure 13.35 is a classic example of a cup with handle pattern. Notice the rounding shape along the lows. This is most often associated with reversals but is more profitable when formed as a continuation pattern. The cup with handle is quite difficult to trade unless the trader is disciplined. This type of pattern will form quite often and can be misleading. To trade it, wait for the breakout and immediately sell the position if it falls below the low of the handle. Experienced investors will see this often. I hate to keep bringing it up, but behavioral biases are everywhere. The exercise that I proposed earlier asking whether the trend was going to continue or reverse was designed to demonstrate that hindsight bias is difficult to overcome. As I seek out these charts to add clarity to the concepts, I am reminded of just how easy it is to succumb to these behaviors that distort reality. Human minds are wired to recognize patterns. I gave examples of this in the behavioral chapter. The most common mistake I see when I mentor other advisors and investors is that they see a pattern such as the cup with handle, and they believe so strongly that the end result will be as I described it. The handle is formed then it breaks out, and investors go all-in only to lose substantial sums of money. Then they give me attitude about these so called patterns I have described to them. First let me say again, minds are wired to see patterns even when they do not exist, so that is the first hurdle to overcome. Next, even when these patterns are legit and all the parameters have been met, they still have a chance of failing, which is an even bigger hurdle. As I said before, the key to a great technician is knowing when a mistake has been made and cutting losses. The mistake is not necessarily the technician's inability to recognize the signals or patterns; the mistake can be the market's. Everything looked great, pattern was traded correctly, but the market changed its mind. Recognizing pattern failures is more important than recognizing the patterns themselves.

The Rounding Top looks like the rounding bottom except it is formed at the top of a bull market rally. When identifying rounding tops and rounding bottoms in individual stock charts, it is important to remember to look to the general market for clues. What I mean is that if the general market is moving higher, and this stock has just formed a rounding bottom, do not anticipate the handle. The handle is nothing more than a throwback as studied in the section on trend lines. If the market is struggling and a stock has just formed a rounding bottom, look for the handle as it suggests the overall market is impacting this stock and could drag it down below the handle which would negate the entire pattern.

Triangles

Triangles can be either continuation patterns or reversal patterns and are by far the most commonly recognized pattern. Since these patterns can be either continuation or reversal, they are also the most unreliable of the patterns. Triangles can form in bear markets as well as bull markets and can be viewed on daily charts as well as weekly charts.

Symmetrical Triangles are best described with a picture as opposed to trying to paint a picture with words. Figure 13.36 displays a typical symmetrical triangle.

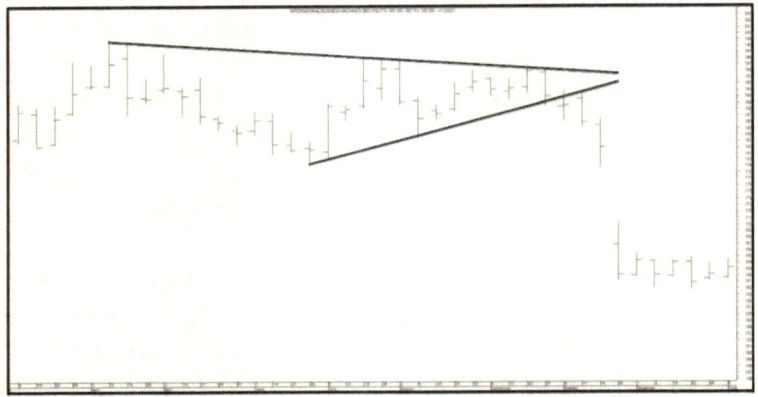

Figure 13.36

The symmetrical triangle can be identified by two trend lines: the resistance trend line slopes downward and the support trend line slopes upward. The problem with symmetrical triangles is they tell investors that the market is indecisive and tension is building, but they fail to show which direction the major move will be, up or down. It is important to watch volume when charting symmetrical triangles as can be seen in Figure 13.37.

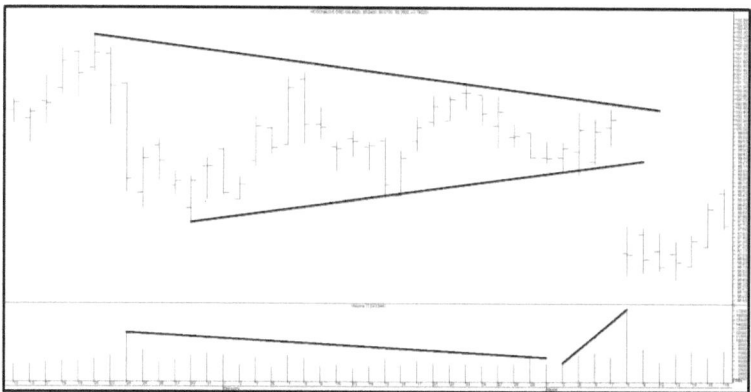

Figure 13.37

As the pattern progresses, each rally in price should be on less and less volume. As the tension builds, volume will typically decline as market participants are unable to determine which direction the price will move. Finally, on the breakout, volume should increase to above normal levels. Sounds so simple I know.

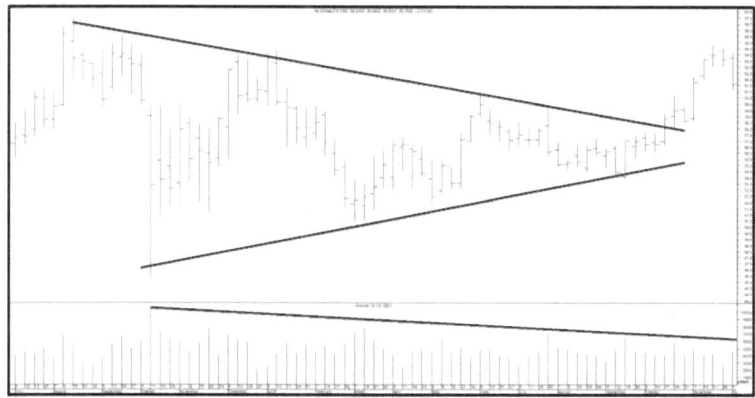

Figure 13.38

Now look at Figure 13.38. The symmetrical triangle forms as normal, but this time with breakout there is no increase in vol‧ume. When discussed earlier, I mentioned volume should be used as a confirmation tool and not as a steadfast rule. This is a perfect example as the triangle is penetrated to the upside, but volume is not there to confirm in this case. If the triangle does not have volume to confirm the move, be ready to exit the position as the price reverses back through the triangle formation. As with trend lines, a breakout is often accompanied by a pullback or throwback into the trend line that was broken. If this occurs and the price bounces off the trend line with increased volume, the trend will likely continue in the direction of the breakout. As demonstrated from the example, these moves are often referred to as *coils*. Symmetrical triangles as with any of the triangles discussed here, the more times the trend lines on both the support and resistance sides are approached or preferably touched, the higher the probability that when a breakout occurs it will be valid. Magee and Edwards state that any breakout in a triangle should follow the same parameters as that of the trend lines we discussed, breakout should be 3% or greater. If the breakout is to the upside, volume is preferred but a breakout to the downside volume is not necessary.

Ascending & Descending Triangles

Also known as Right Triangles, the Ascending and Descending Triangles are similar to the Symmetrical Triangle but offer a hint at the direction the market will likely take after the breakout.

MCDONALD'S ORD (90.9600, 94.3200, 87.6200, 93.2200, +2.60000)

Figure 13.39

Figure 13.39 shows an Ascending Triangle and the breakout to the upside. The difference between the symmetrical triangle and the Right triangle is in the support and resistance lines that make up the triangle. The Symmetrical Triangle has both a sloping resistance and a sloping support trend line. They converge toward each other. The Right Triangle on the other hand has either a horizontal support or resistance line while the opposite trend line slopes toward the other trend line. Figure 13.39 shows an Ascending Triangle where the resistance trend line is horizontal and the support trend line slopes upward toward resistance. The great thing about Right Triangles is the hint they provide the technical analyst as to the direction the price should go after the breakout. An Ascending Triangle is typically bullish and should breakout to the upside. The Ascending Triangle displays in great fashion the supply and demand of a stock. The resistance trend line typically holds since a number of sellers of the stock want out at this fixed price. The buyers on the other hand continue to be willing to pay more in each advance than in the previous. Once the supply has been absorbed by new buy orders, the price breaks out of the Ascending Triangle since demand for the stock now exceeds that of the sellers.

Figure 13.40

Figure 13.40 shows a Descending Triangle and the breakout that follows. The Descending Triangle is identical to the Ascending Triangle except the trend lines have switched roles. Now the resistance slopes toward the support line and the breakout is to the downside. This of course is a bearish indicator, but in my studies of technical patterns, I have found there to be a high failure rate among this particular pattern. I have found it to be a consolidation pattern more times than a bearish reversal pattern.

Figure 13.41

Figure 13.41 displays the failure of a Descending Triangle. Everything looks typical of the Descending Triangle until it breaks to the upside, moves more than 3%, and then throws-back to the now support trend line that was once the downward sloping trend line before shooting to new highs. Volume is identical for the Right Triangles as it is for the Symmetrical Triangles. As the pattern progresses, there is a slowdown in volume until the breakout, which should then be on higher volume if to the upside.

As we move through the typical classic patterns, notice that most patterns tend to somewhat anticipate a stock's price target after the pattern is completed. The triangle pattern is no exception.

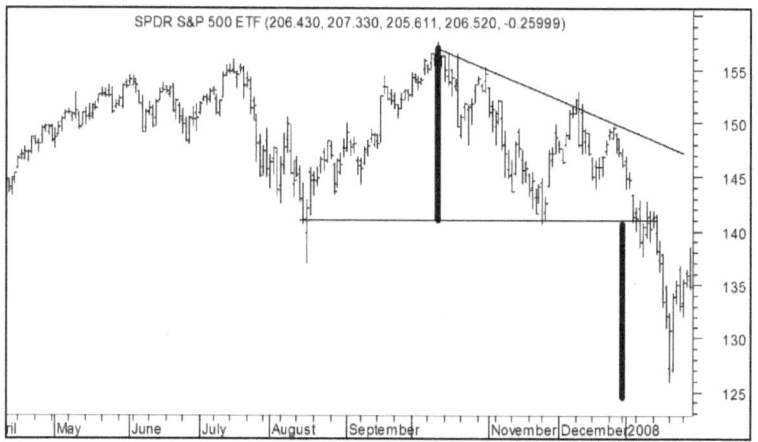

Figure 13.42

To compute a price target from the triangle pattern, calculate the price spread of the triangle at its widest point which is the beginning of the pattern. As demonstrated in Figure 13.42, use this spread calculation and extend it in the direction of the breakout. This will give an idea as to where to expect the price to move after the pattern has completed.

Rectangles

Rectangles are one of my favorite patterns, not because they are more reliable than other patterns but because they typically represent a consolidation as opposed to a reversal and are easier to identify. I would have to offer a cautionary word at this juncture. Often at the beginning of a Rectangle, it looks as though a triangle is forming. The triangle pattern is broken, but the price does not make new highs or new lows and stays within the boundaries of the first peak and trough. At this point, transition from thinking the triangle pattern has completed, which it has, to the fact that this new information gives guidance as to the current and correct pattern. Once the new pattern has been identified as a Rectangle, look at prior price history to see the direction of the trend before the pattern. If the primary trend was up, assume the trend will continue once the Rectangle is complete. Investors must remain vigilant though because the Rectangle can also fail like any other patterns previously studied. Another drawback to the Rectangle is that the price goes nowhere, and this pattern can last for weeks or even months.

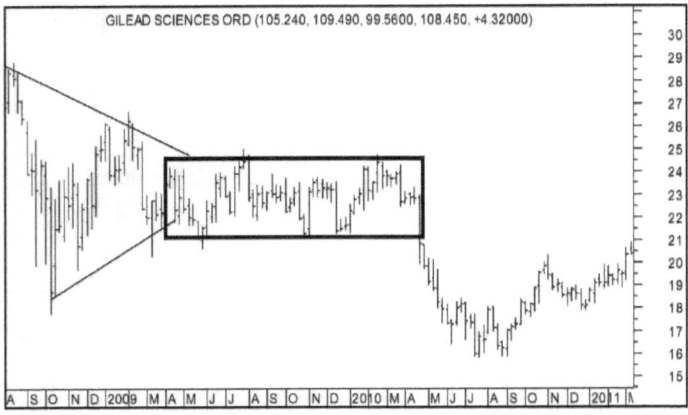

Figure 13.43

Figure 13.43 displays what was explained above: before the Rectangle formed, the identifiable pattern was a triangle. If the triangle trend lines had been extended, it was possible to notice that the triangle was violated to the downside before rallying upwards and violating to the upside. It may not be clear to the beginner technician to even watch for the rectangle. At times this is when frustration sets in, especially if the violations of the triangle involve losses of capital. The experienced investor looks ahead and tries to anticipate the next move and will likely realize early that the triangle is leading to another pattern. The above figure shows the consolidation and the eventual breakout to the downside. Volume on the rectangle is identical to volume on triangles in that volume typically decreases as the pattern moves through time only to pick up on the breakout.

Broadening Triangles

Broadening Triangles look like any other triangle previously discussed except the apex is at the beginning and the pattern moves wider the further out it moves. Figure 13.44 gives an example of the Broadening Triangle.

Figure 13.44

Magee and Edwards have said that Broadening Triangles "suggest a market is lacking intelligent sponsorship and is out of control." We are currently experiencing history in the making. If reading this book decades from the year it was published (2015), recall studying the "Great Recession" of 2008. As I was preparing to write this chapter, I came across the above statement that Magee and Edwards wrote decades before. The year 2014 ended what has become known as Quantitative Easing. What this means is that after the 2008 financial crisis, the Federal Reserve decided that in order to avoid a depression, the treasury must print money to provide liquidity to the markets. This has created some interesting valuations in the markets. The usual fundamental indicators of economic growth and improvement appear to have been put on hold as investors try to digest just what all this liquidity means in the markets. On some metrics, this market is extremely overvalued and on others metrics it appears fairly valued. One thing is certain at this time: the markets are not undervalued. Since the Tech Bubble burst in the early 2000s and the Financial Crisis of 2008, the market is once again at all-time highs. Some investors may not realize that the market is in the midst of a multiyear broadening formation shown in Figure 13.45.

Figure 13.45

As demonstrated from the broadening top in Figure 13.45, the market is at an inflection point. Years from now, it will be known whether the formation held true, and the markets corrected significantly or whether this was a failed pattern. As with all price patterns only time will tell. Looking at a pattern such as the one in Figure 13.45, investors must remain rational and not believe too strongly that the outcome of a pattern will go exactly as planned. Because there is a pattern such as that in Figure 13.45, does not mean that this pattern is true and that investors should short the market. Large sums of money have been lost to such foolishness.

The last two classic patterns under discussion are the Flag and the Pennant. Both of these patterns are usually continuation patterns and can be highly profitable when used correctly. The Flag and Pennant are identical, and their interpretations are the same, the only difference is the pennant resembles a wedge pattern and the flag more of a rectangle or sometimes a slanted rectangle that can slope upward or downward and this does not affect meaning. Figures 13.46 represents a Flag and 13.47 represents a Pennant.

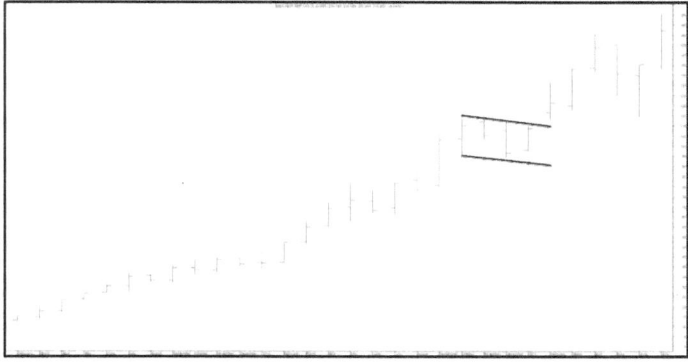

Figure 13.46

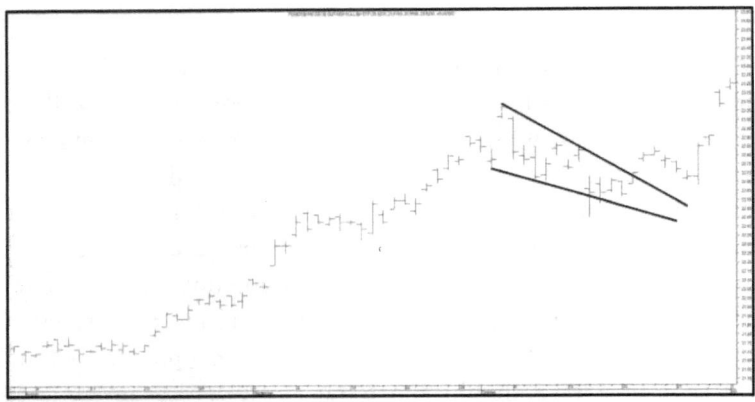

Figure 13.47

When comparing these two patterns there really is little difference between the two, and it is not necessary to take the time
studying the minute differences. It is necessary to understand
that these patterns are consolidation or continuation patterns
with another common characteristic that is extremely useful.
Once a Flag or Pennant has been identified, it signals that this
is the halfway point in the move. This can be a great advantage when studying high momentum stocks. Instead of trying to identify reversal patterns, focus on Flags and Pennants
to signal addition profits to be made. When most investors see
a stock such as the one in Figure 13.47, they falsely believe the
Pennant or Flag is indicating that the price is reversing. If
they were more astute to price patterns, they might not exit
trades early and thereby miss impressive gains to come.

[14]

Technical Statistics

With a basic knowledge of price patterns investors or analysts have the foundation for technical analysis. There are several books on the basics which are extremely important. Two personal favorites are *Technical Analysis Explained,* by Martin Pring, and *Technical Analysis of Stock Trends,* by Robert Edwards and John Magee. Both these books will provide an in-depth explanation of price patterns with more precise detail. The intention of this book is not another look at technical analysis but rather to offer an understanding of its importance and place within a sound investment strategy.

As demonstrated from the study of price patterns, this was an introduction to charting and price recognition. It was not until the advent and popularity of the computer that technical statistics were used as an investment tool. Relative Strength nor Momentum are heavily discussed in *Technical Analysis of Stock Trends* since that book was first written in the 1940s. Any book written post computer age will spend more time on technical statistics as opposed to price patterns. I believe that price patterns are the foundation from which technical statistics are drawn and understanding the patterns offers a better grasp than the statistical components. This chapter will cover the most common technical indicators and will avoid the more math intensive statistics. This chapter will cover Relative Strength, Moving Average Convergence Divergence (MACD), and Momentum. It is imperative to be careful when implementing more than one "momentum" indicator as there is the possibility of creating an environment of multicollinearity.

Relative Strength Index (RSI)

The Relative Strength Index is the most misunderstood indicator in my opinion. The RSI indicator was developed by Wells Wilder and is classified as an oscillator. The formula for calculating RSI is:

$$RSI = 100 - \frac{(100)}{1+RS}$$

Where RS is equal to the average n days' up closes divided by the average of n days' down closes.

A general understanding of RSI will confirm that the RSI is normally thought of as an indicator that tells an investor when a security is overbought or oversold. Look at Figure 14.1.

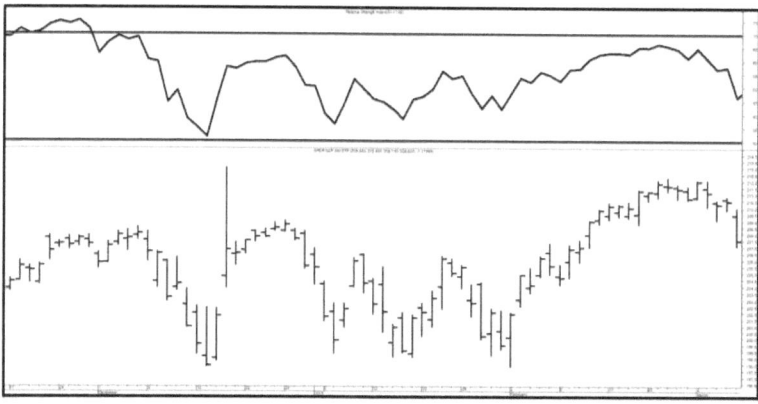

Figure 14.1

Figure 14.1 shows the RSI plotted above the price chart. The bottom horizontal line is fixed at 30 and the top horizontal line is fixed at 70. It is generally taught that when a stock's RSI moves above 70, it is overbought and when it falls to 30 it is oversold. This appears to be an accurate depiction. As the stock bounces off the 30 level, it begins to move higher until it reaches the overbought level of 70 and then falls in value. This looks like a wise way to invest. However, if an investor follows this method, it would soon become apparent that there are several instances where the stock becomes overbought but does not fall to the oversold level for long periods of time. This also happens on the downside. A stock becomes oversold based on RSI only to stay in an almost neutral state for several days to several months. Figure 14.2 is an example of this miscalibration of the RSI.

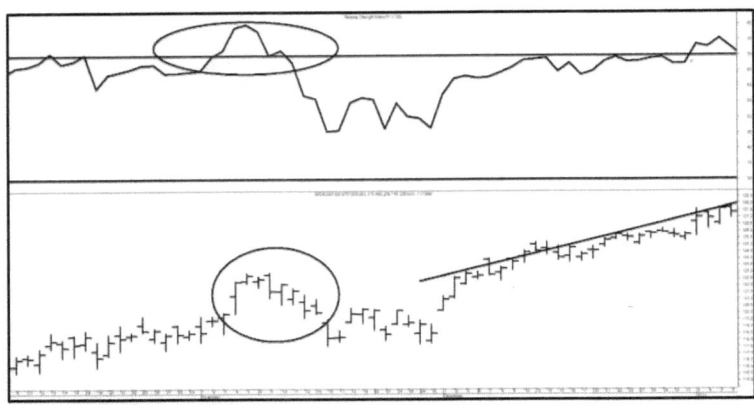

Figure 14.2

Following the above RSI trading rules results in a missed rally that followed due to the RSI giving an overbought signal and not returning to an oversold as the price trend continued to move higher. Recall from the chapter on behavioral investing that the pain of a loss is about twice as strong as the joy from an equal sized gain. A close study of Figure 14.2 may cause the investor to think, "Well I still made a profit." This is true. Now look at Figure 14.3.

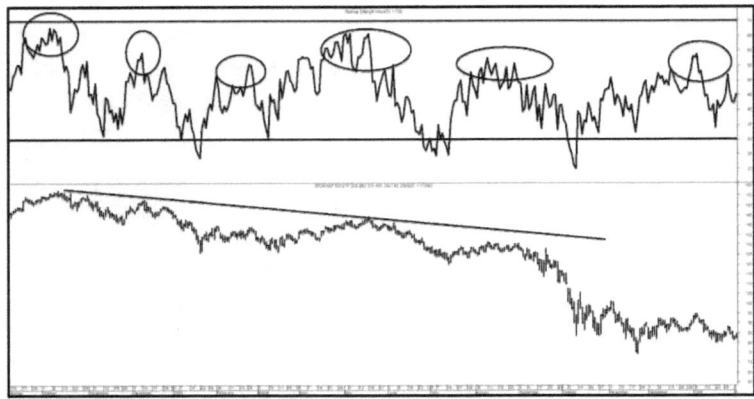

Figure 14.3

This time the role is reversed, and the investors bought into a stock and were unable to get reliable indication as to when to exit the long position. Each time the RSI moved to oversold, an investor likely chose to stay with it because the price was going to bounce. The price did bounce but failed to make new highs or even recoup the earlier losses. This often leads to frustration and abandonment of the RSI indicator.

What I am going to teach in the remainder of this section is an alternative way to interpret the RSI. This is not new but is often overlooked when beginning a journey of technical analysis. I have read the basic premise in Constanance Brown's book called *Technical Analysis for the Trading Professional* and have read similar interpretations.

Figure 14.3a is the same chart as Figure 14.3 except for the light grey horizontal line at 65 in the RSI indicator.

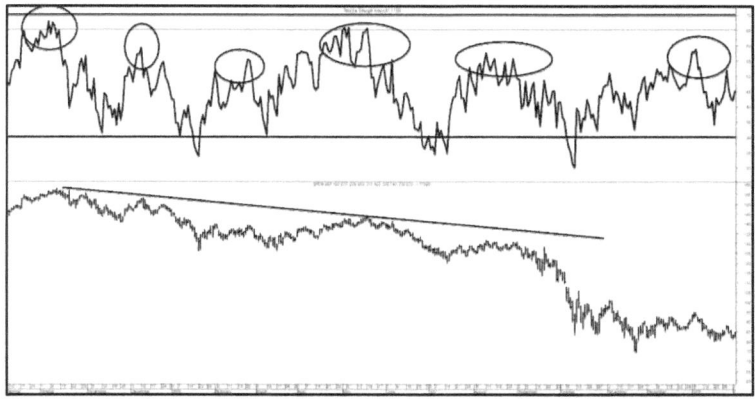

Figure 14.3a

When a stock is in a downtrend, it will often fall short of the overbought level of 70 and will often stay in the range of 60 to 65. The oversold condition does not change as demonstrated in Figure 14.3a. Each time the market makes a lower high and a lower low, the RSI fails to break the overbought condition which is a signal that the trend is down, and the RSI indicator should not be used in the same oversold and overbought manner. Look at an uptrend and how the RSI responds.

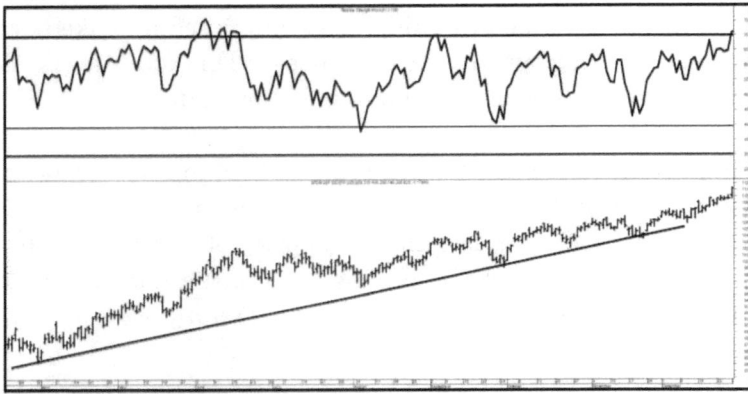

Figure 14.4

Figure 14.4 is an example of an uptrend and the readings on the RSI indicator. To identify an uptrend using RSI, monitor each higher low and higher high of the trend. When the RSI is only falling to around 40 (represented by the light gray horizontal line in the RSI indicator) before turning upward and the price is making higher highs, the uptrend has been identified. This may seem like it is a late indicator and it is. An investor can use this type analysis to stay in a position or to refrain from entering a new position during a downtrend.

This is not the only use for the RSI. Many technicians monitor the RSI for divergences between RSI trend and price trend. If a stock's price makes new highs but he RSI fails to make a new high, this could be a signal that the trend is nearing the end and an investor should focus on when to exit.

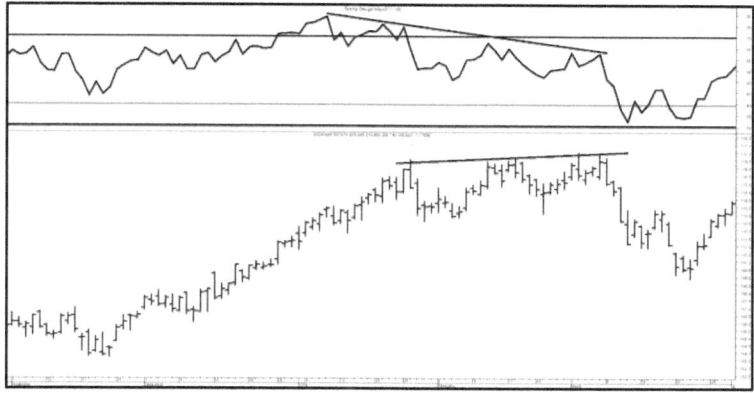

Figure 14.5

Figure 14.5 gives an example of what is labeled as a negative divergence. The stock's price has continued to make new highs whereas the RSI has failed to follow suit. This indicates that the underlying strength of this trend is weakening and an investor should take notice.

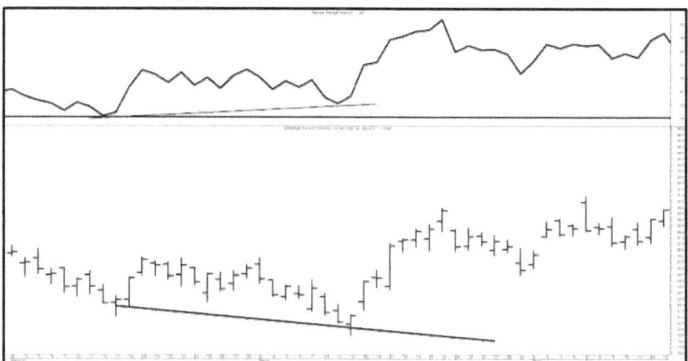

Figure 14.6

If there is a negative divergence, there also a positive divergence. Figure 14.6 represents this. When the price makes a new low, but the RSI fails to do the same, there is a positive divergence telling us that selling pressure is being overcome by buying pressure, and the downtrend may be coming to an end.

This should give potential investors a good overview of the RSI indicator and why it is often misused or at least not used to its full capacity. Remember all indicators and interpretations will fail from time to time. This should not be a point of frustration but a learning experience. The RSI indicator is an indispensable tool in technical analysis because of its multifaceted capabilities.

Moving Average Convergence Divergence (MACD)

One of the most popular technical indicators is the MACD. This momentum indicator was developed by Gerald Appel in the 1970s and nearly any investor whether a technician or not will probably know what is being discussed when MACD is mentioned. MACD is in the same category as RSI; it is a momentum indicator. Keep in mind that momentum is a generic term in technical analysis just as Ford, Lincoln and Mercury can represent the general term for car.

MACD uses two exponential moving averages that can be customized to the investor's time horizon. Instead of using the moving averages as in the crossover strategy, subtract the short-term moving average from the long-term moving average and plot this difference. Most investors find it useful to plot the difference as a histogram that moves above and below zero. Then a third moving average called the signal line is plotted separately. The moving averages used are exponential moving averages which weigh more recent periods more heavily than older periods. Metastock uses a 12-day exponential subtracted from a 26-day exponential moving average to create the convergence/divergence histogram, and a 9-day exponential moving average as the signal line. These moving averages can be adjusted to suit any investor's time horizon. More information on how to manipulate moving averages to construct a more appropriate MACD is available in my article published in Technical Analysis of Stocks and Commodities titled "Trading Momentum."

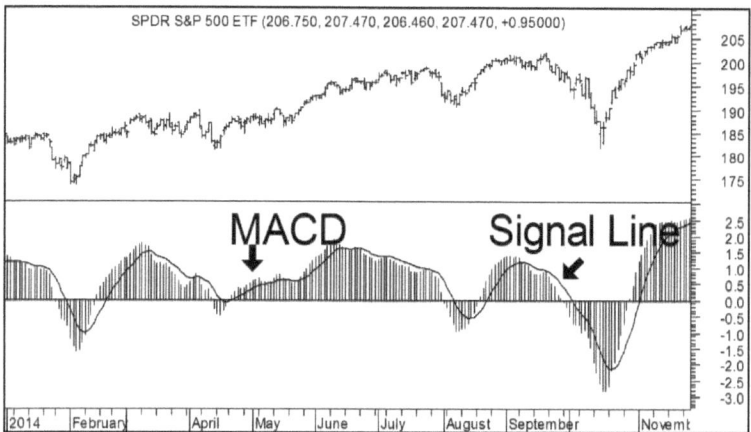

Figure 14.7

Figure 14.7 shows the MACD at work. As the histogram begins to fade lower, this signals a slowing of momentum and should not be misunderstood for a change in price trend. MACD should be thought of mathematically. As the fast moving average moves further away from the slow moving average, there is divergence or a larger spread in the numbers. A larger spread in the moving average indicates the fast moving average is rising faster than the slow moving average and momentum is gaining speed. As the slow moving average stalls or reverses, the slow moving average may still be climbing. This creates the convergence and the spread narrows. This narrowing of the spread is indicated on the chart as a slowing of momentum. This MACD can be used to trade in a number of ways. The first way to analyze MACD is to sell a position if the MACD histogram falls below the signal line as shown in Figure 14.8.

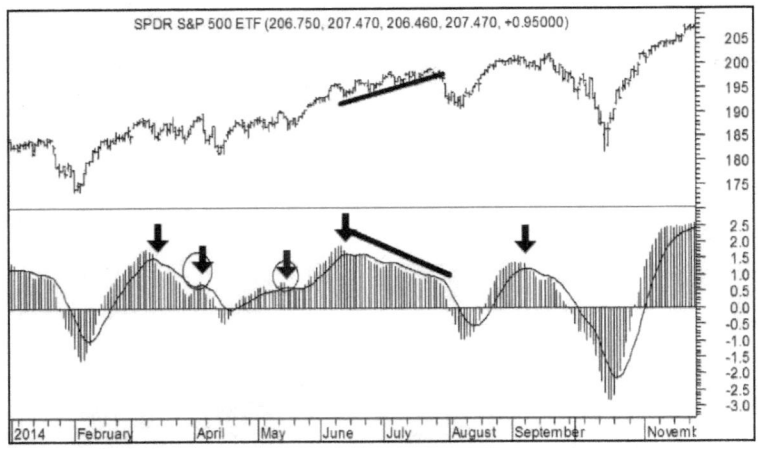

SPDR S&P 500 ETF (206.750, 207.470, 206.460, 207.470, +0.95000)

Figure 14.8

There are multiple lessons to be learned from this chart alone. The first arrow pointing downward represents a typical sell signal that is taught to beginner technicians. But there are several false signals using this method and most investors become frustrated due to losses and missed gains. The two arrows with circles are the typical whipsaw trades as can be expected using any form of momentum. MACD however, tends to create more false signals than most indicators I have studied. Next I want to draw attention to the long thick lines on the chart. This is a situation where the momentum of price has slowed down but the trend remains intact. If an investor would have traded at this signal he or she would have likely missed a decent rally. These false moves often lead investors to distrust the indicator namely because they do not understand it well in the first place. Momentum indicators such as MACD *can* be early indicators of a trend reversal but should not be used as hard fast buy and sell rules. I think that many authors of books, myself included, expect beginners to intuitively understand the basics and therefore use words such as "buy" and "sell" signal in place of more appropriate words such as "possible signal." The investor must keep in mind that technical analysis is not a science and therefore a signal should never be mistaken for fact or guarantee of success.

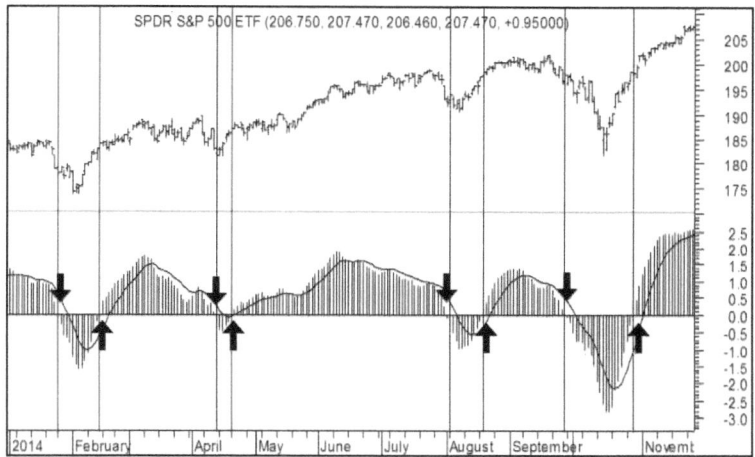

Figure 14.9

Another approach for determining "possible" buy and sell signals is illustrated in Figure 14.9. A buy signal is triggered when the histogram crosses above the zero line and a sell signal is triggered when it falls below the same zero line. The vertical lines in Figure 14.9 represent the approximate price level when each of the signals occurred, and as shown there is not a single signal that benefits the investor during this time period. Each time a sell signal was triggered, a buy signal was triggered at a higher price. Frustration would have probably destroyed investors' confidence if they had traded each signal.

I have consulted with several advisors over the years on the use of technical analysis to benefit a client's portfolio returns over the long-term. Most have stated that they "tried it a couple times" but in the long run were not successful. This tells me they were likely using standard "buy" and "sell" signals such as the ones in Figure 14.9. I have also heard over the years advisors wanting to implement a "sell discipline" in their investment strategy. Again the best sell discipline is useless without an equally strong buy discipline. What they were telling me was that they wanted to be able to sell out of positions before they lost money using technical analysis. I have had to explain more times than I want to recall that technical analysis if not used properly can harm a portfolio by selling out of positions when it was not prudent to do so just as detrimentally as not selling out of losing positons entirely. This is why it is key to understand what drives the indicators. Long-term value investors may want to study MACD using a weekly or monthly chart.

MACD is an important indicator to measure momentum but should not be used for entry and exit points but rather for confirmation as depicted in Figure 14.10 below.

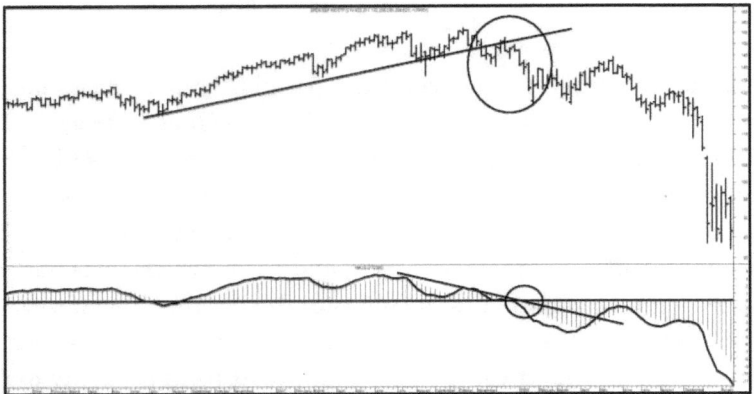

Figure 14.10

As indicated in Figure 14.10, about the time the MACD crosses zero, an upward trend line is violated to the downside, this provides confirmation that the trend line break is valid and should be acted upon. The downward sloping trend line in the MACD chart also provides confirmation of the price trend line break.

Martin Pring uses the motto, "Weight of the Evidence." Which means investors and analysts must continue to look for evidence and make a decision based on the weight of the evidence the charts are providing. For this reason MACD adds value as an additional weight to add indicator evidence.

The MACD as with any oscillating indicator can be interpreted using different methods such as looking for patterns within the indicator like triangles or trend lines by looking for divergences with price and even something as simple as looking for extreme levels. The key to successfully implementing technical analysis is to study the indicators extensively before attempting to trust them without emotional biases. Failure to do this will be setting an investor up for frustration and failure.

Stochastics

Stochastic is a term used in statistics which by definition means, having a random probability distribution or pattern that may be analyzed statistically but may not be predicted precisely. This is truly a fitting definition for a technical indicator or for investing in general. The stochastic indicator does not accurately depict the above definition. The Stochastic indicator is another form of momentum and has become quite popular with short-term traders since the underlying formula uses short-term time spans. George Lane, the inventor of the Stochastic oscillator theorized that when a stock is in an uptrend, the price of that stock will tend to close near the highs, and when an uptrend is losing steam, the price will tend to vary and close away from the higher end of the range. The opposite would hold true in a downward move. Figure 14.11 shows the Stochastic Oscillator at work.

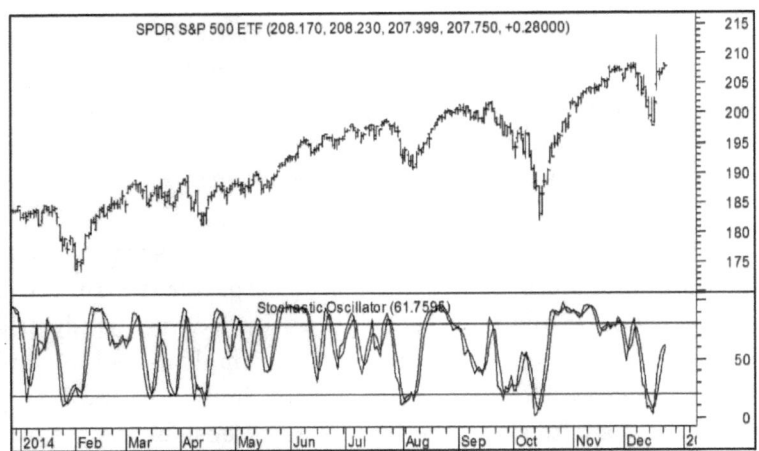

SPDR S&P 500 ETF (208.170, 208.230, 207.399, 207.750, +0.28000)

Stochastic Oscillator (61.7596)

Figure 14.11

As the price begins to close away from the direction of the underlying trend, the stochastic will reverse indicating the next move is in the opposite direction. As with any other indicator, the timeframe used is of utmost importance. The stochastic oscillator performs rather poorly when compared to the other indicators and strategies covered in this book according to Colby and Meyers, in *The Encyclopedia of Technical Market Indicators* (McGraw-Hill 2002). In his book *Technical Analysis Explained,* Martin Pring developed a special case of the stochastic oscillator known as Special K and has covered extensively the many methods and concepts of the Stochastic oscillator.

There are so many indicators today that it would be a full time job trying to keep up with the new indicators that are introduced to the investing world every year. The industry recently introduced High Frequency Trading, HFT, where supercomputers use algorithms to produce trades in fractions of seconds. These algorithms are simply another form of technical analysis. I wrote this chapter not as an attempt to explain everything I know or have read about technical analysis but to give an idea as to how to use technical analysis in an overall invest-ment strategy. I do not expect an investor to read this book and attempt to day trade with large blocks of money; however, I hope that an investor gains enough knowledge to apply these concepts to an overall investment strategy whether doing it as an individual or as an advisor wanting to add a unique ability that will set him or her apart from other advisors. I have only mentioned the "big" three in momentum indicators and there are several hundred more. Maybe a more comprehensive tech-nical analysis book will follow this edition.

Market Breadth

Most books on technical analysis include a chapter on the sub-ject of market breadth, including this book. However, Greg Morris has dedicated an entire book to the subject called "The Complete Guide to Market Breadth Indicators." I will attempt to give a broad overview of market breadth as well as some of the most popular indicators. A close read of Morris' book will provide an in-depth analysis of the subject.

Market breadth indicators are generally described as an at-tempt to measure the overall health of the markets. Breadth indicators typically use only a few pieces of data. Morris (2006) used the following definitions for the data used to develop mar-ket breadth indicators:

Advancing Issues: Stocks that have increased in price from one day to the next, even if only by 1 cent are considered as advancing issues or advances.

Declining Issues: Stocks that have decreased in price from one day to the next are considered declining issues or declines.

Unchanged Issues or Unchanged: Stocks that do not change in price from one day to the next are considered unchanged issues or unchanged.

Total Issues: Total of all issues available for trading on a particular exchange. Adding the advances, declines, and unchanged issues together will equal the total issues.

Advancing Volume or Up Volume: The volume traded on a day for each of the stocks that are advancing issues. It is the total volume of all the advances.

Declining Volume or Down Volume: The total volume for all the declines for a particular day.

Total Volume: The total volume of all trading for a particular day.

New High: A stock's price reaches a new high price for the last 52-weeks.

New Low: A stock's price reaches a new low price for the last 52-weeks.

Market breadth uses this data to determine if investors are buying or selling stocks and also investigates their conviction. Market breadth looks at the entire market under analysis such as the New York Stock Exchange (NYSE) and determines if more stocks were bought than sold and how many issues changed hands. Breadth equally weighs all stocks within the index so it provides better unbiased data about the health of market moves. Most market indexes are either price weighted or market cap weighted so they can be manipulated by a few large companies. Market breadth eliminates this bias and more precisely represents the markets. A penny stock has as much weight as Apple when analyzing market breadth.

Rather than trying to recreate what Mr. Morris has already perfected, I will summarize the most popular breadth indicators. First, Let us look at the Advance Decline line.

The Advance Decline Line was created by Colonel Leaonard P. Ayres and is one of the most basic and popular market breadth indicators. All that is need to calculate this indictor are advancing issues data and declining issues data from a market or exchange. Mr. Ayres subtracted the declining issues from the advancing issues each day, and if the advances outnumber the declines, the net difference is added to the previous total or subtracted if the declines outnumber the advances. This is a simple indicator and is easy to read. If there are more advances than declines, the line goes up; if there are more declines than advances the line goes down. Simple, right? The Advance Decline Line (ADL) is best used when comparing the index that is associated with the breadth data. The most common way to interpret the ADL is to look for divergences. Such as if the ADL makes a new high and the associated index fails to make a new high, pay attention as this could be a warning that the trend is not as strong as it may appear.

Morris describes the primary value in using the ADL is its relationship to liquidity. When there is ample liquidity in the markets, it tends to be spread around to more issues and therefore will be indicated in the breadth statistics. This shows the direct comparison to supply and demand in the overall markets.

The final breadth indicator under consideration is the McClellan Oscillator developed by husband and wife team, Sherman and Marian McClellan. The McClellan Oscillator takes the difference between the 19-day and the 39-day exponential moving averages of the daily net advances minus declines.

The interpretation is somewhat similar to the relative strength index as it attempts to identify oversold and overbought conditions. When the indicator registers +100, a short-term overbought signal is given and when the indicator reaches -100, a short-term oversold signal is given. However, if the indicator reaches +130 or -130, the signals can be interpreted quite differently. When the oscillator drops to -130 and begins to rally this can be a secondary sell signal as the rally often fails. The same is true for a reading of +130. Sherman McClellan says that readings in the -125 to -130 range are often an early indication of even more selling pressure to come due to the markets becoming illiquid. Figure 14.12 shows the McClellan Oscillator at work.

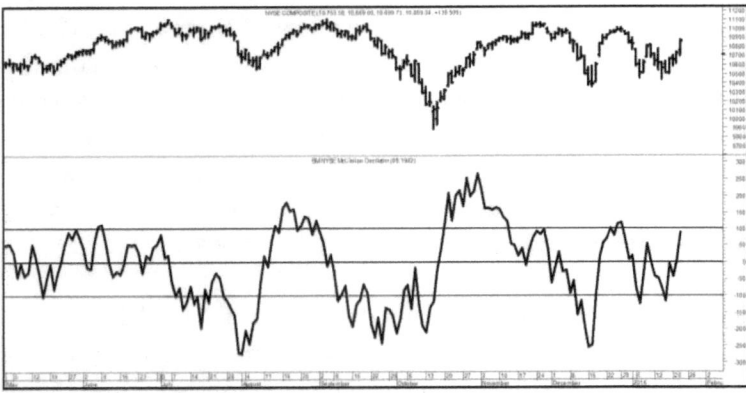

Figure 14.12

Market Breadth indicators can add an entirely new dimension to an overall investment strategy. Market breadth is often overlooked and misunderstood which is why it does not receive the attention it deserves. It is amazing that only a handful of data points can give so much information about the health of the markets. As I mentioned before, an in-depth look at market breadth indicators is available in Greg Morris' book which will give a complete understanding and a new appreciation for market breadth indicators.

[15]

Advanced Techniques

Elliott Wave Theory

I will give fair warning that once read, this section on Elliott Wave will forever change an investor. This could be for the good or the bad. An investor will, after completing and studying the pages that follow, count the waves on every chart. This is fine, but do not succumb to the temptation of believing in a personal ability to actually predict market moves. Elliott wave is a tantalizing tool and is often criticized for leaving too much to interpretation. Any given chart pattern can be interpreted many different ways.

Ralph Nelson Elliott believed that stock market prices moved in recognizable trends and patterns. He believed that this market structure was characterized by waves that varied in length and in time. A single wave structure is composed of an impulse wave and a corrective wave. The corrective wave does exactly that: goes against the current trend. Impulse waves are generally labeled with numbers and are composed of five subwaves, of which waves 1, 3, and 5 are in the direction of the prevailing trend and waves 2 and 4 are the corrective waves. Figure 14.1 gives an example of a simple wave structure.

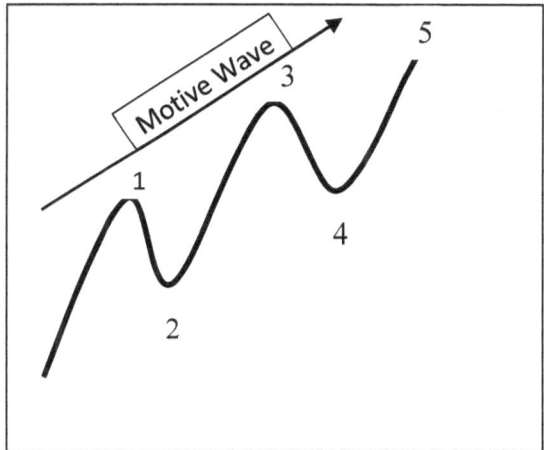

Figure 15.1

Each impulse subwave is composed of five waves of a lesser degree. So the first wave in Figure 15.1 has a five wave struc-ture of one lesser degree. This can be seen in Figure 15.2 be-low. The impulse waves up and the corrective waves down are now broken into their respective subwaves. The labeling of the waves is not important. Many Elliott practitioners label waves with numbers or letters or roman numerals. All that matters is that an investor is able to keep track of each label and its organizational properties.

There are rules that wave counts and wave structures must adhere. If any of the rules are violated, the entire wave count is invalid. Robert Pretcher and A.J. Frost in their book *Elliott Wave Principle*, outline rules that must be adhered to as well as guidelines that help with interpretation and identification. The rules from their book are listed below:

Impulse Wave Rules:

- An impulse always subdivides into five waves.
- Wave 1 always subdivides into impulse or (rarely) a diagonal.
- Wave 3 always subdivides into an impulse wave.
- Wave 5 always subdivides into an impulse or a diagonal
- Wave 2 always subdivides onto a zigzag, flat, or combination (we will address these patterns shortly)
- Wave 4 always subdivides into a zigzag, flat , triangle, or combination.
- Wave 2 never moves beyond the start of wave 1.
- Wave 3 always moves beyond the end of wave 1
- Wave 3 is never the shortest wave.
- Wave 4 never moves beyond the end of wave 1.
- Never are waves 1, 3, and 5 all extended.

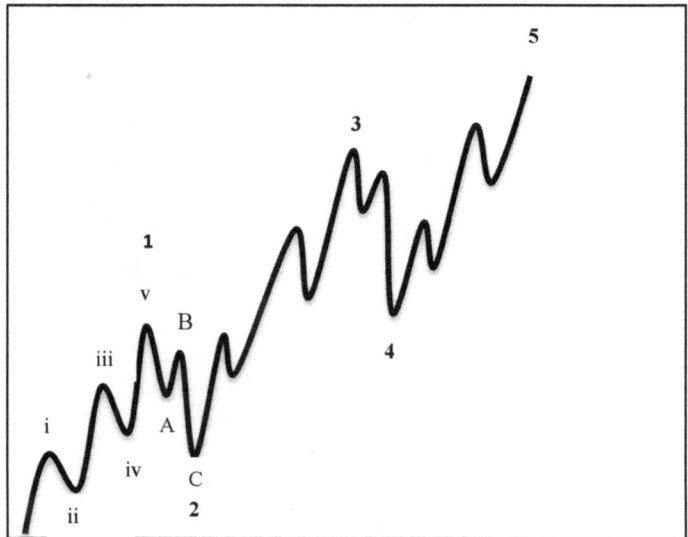

Figure 15.2

Corrective Waves

Unlike the simple structure of an impulse wave, corrective waves are often misinterpreted and difficult to label since they form many different patterns. Corrective waves occur in three waves often labeled, A, B, C. There are only a few corrective wave patterns, but even with so few patterns, their structure often causes confusion. Typical corrective waves are called, zigzags, flats, and triangles and can occur in combinations of the three. Figure 15.3 displays the zigzag pattern in single and double capacity. Figure 15.4 displays the corrective flat patterns.

As discussed in the Dow Theory and the chapter on trend lines, it is only through great effort that the primary trend is reversed. This is possibly the reason the corrective waves of Elliott Wave Theory (EWT) have a difficult time creating identifiably structured patterns. The Zigzag pattern generally follows the wave structure of 5-3-5. The 5 in 5-3-5 is an impulse wave structure and the 3 is a corrective wave structure. In figure 15.3A the A wave in the simple zigzag pattern would subdivide into five waves, the B would subdivide into three waves and the C would subdivide into five ways like the A wave. The Zigzag can occur up to a maximum of three times, back to back. This will usually happen when the first Zigzag fails to make it to the anticipated price target.

If however tracking a corrective wave lower and the first leg down only subdivides into three waves, it is likely to be a flat as shown in Figure 15.4. The Flat wave structure is 3-3-5 which differs from the Zigzag in the first wave down. The Flat often lacks enough force to create the five wave structure. This causes wave C to end around the low of wave A. There is another Flat pattern with the same 3-3-5 wave structure, however wave B moves beyond the start of wave A. This wave

structure is known as an Expanded Flat. Often times begin‐
ning Elliott Wave practitioners will mistake this wave struc‐
ture as a failure when the B wave moves beyond the wave A.

The Triangle wave structure is 3‐3‐3‐3‐3. The Triangle is sim‐
ilar to the triangle we studied in the Classic Pattern chapter.
The only difference is that in EWT investors are looking for a
specific wave structure as opposed to peak and trough points.
The Triangle represented in Figure 15.5 is composed of three
wave structures in a five wave up move.

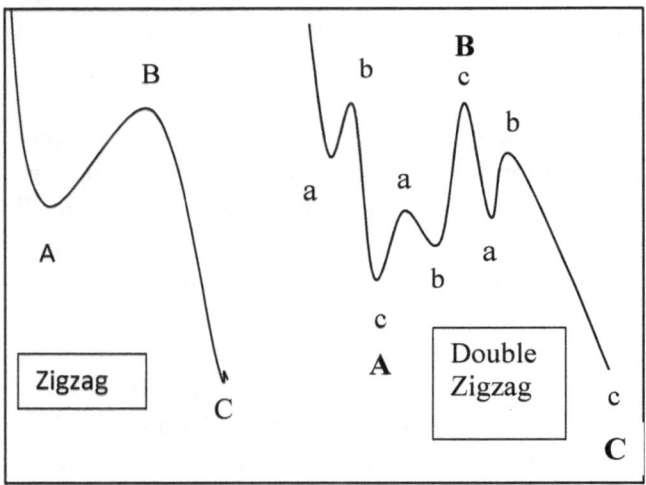

Figure 15.3

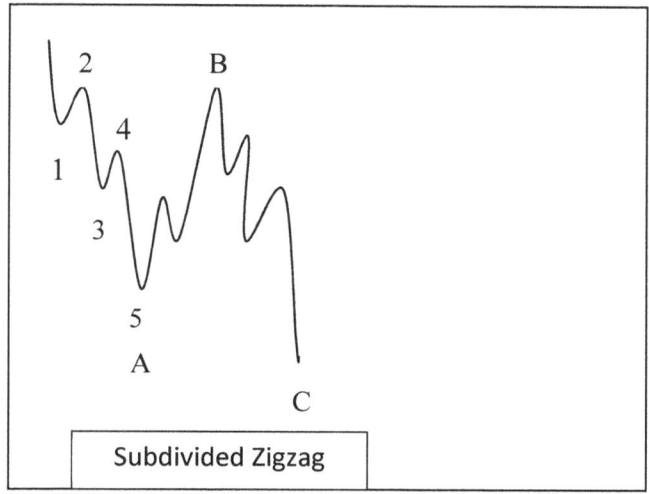

Figure 15.3A

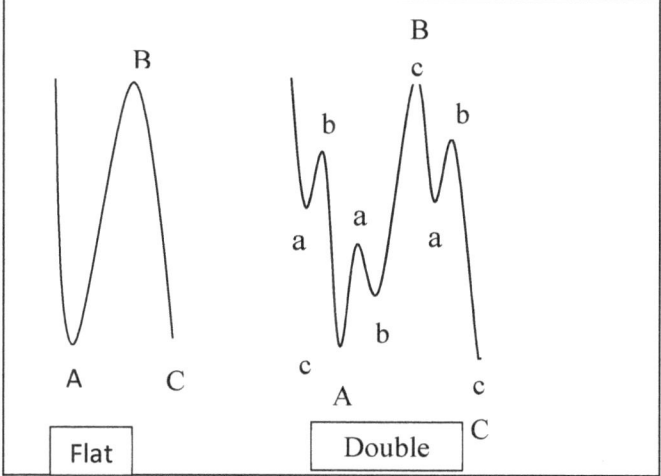

Figure 15.4

In a Double Flat and a Double Zigzag, the labeling A-B-C is often changed to X-Y-Z to avoid confusion as to what degree the wave is unfolding. In Figure 15.4 and 15.3, I chose to use upper and lower case letters to represent what degree the wave structure was in. The X-Y-Z is present in other literature but remember the labeling is used to determine the degree of the current wave.

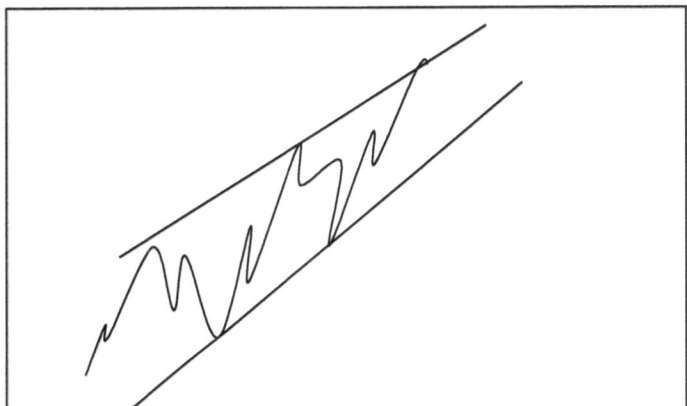

Figure 15.5

The Triangle waves are labeled A-B-C-D-E and can be in the form of right-angle triangles, expanding triangles, and the typical symmetrical triangles. Pretcher and Frost assert Triangles invariably occur prior to the final wave in a move of one larger degree such as wave four in an impulse, and wave B in an A-B-C.

There are often characteristics of certain wave structures that help the practitioner determine what wave structure is currently unfolding and what can be expected in the waves going forward. The wave A of a Zigzag will generally be an impulse wave, a leading diagonal, or a simple zigzag. Wave B is the corrective wave within a corrective pattern. Wave C will likely be an impulse or ending diagonal and can also be a zigzag.

The Flats which are generally sideways patterns often have characteristics very similar to the zigzag other than Wave B cannot be a Triangle and it must also retrace at least 50% of wave A. Wave C must overlap wave A at some point in the corrective move.

General Guidelines of EWT

The guidelines of EWT are not inviolate as are the rules and at times these guidelines will fail. In this section, I will review the guidelines that are often found in EWT.

Alternation in EWT means if tracking a wave pattern and see‐ing one type of corrective wave in the number 2 wave of an impulse, expect that a different corrective wave will form in wave 4. For example, if wave 2 is a Zigzag, look for wave 4 to be a Flat or Triangle. The guideline of impulse wave correc‐tions can also be applied to corrective waves.

In impulse wave structures expect to see waves 1 and 5 are nearly equal in length. It can be other waves that exhibit the equality of waves, but 1 and 5 are the most common.

Prechter has identified several interesting guidelines that help tremendously in identifying where a move can potentially end. One of particular great use is the wave 4 correction price tar‐get. Wave 4 will often correct to wave 4 of one lessor degree and should not move past the low of the previous wave 4 as shown in Figure 15.6.

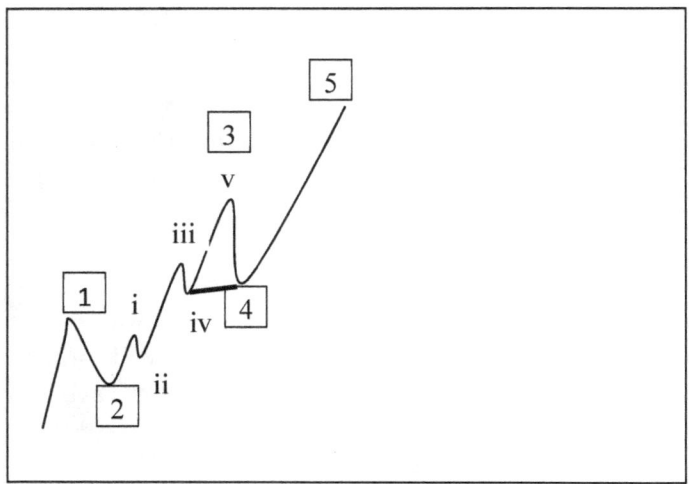

Figure 15.6

There are several books on Elliott Wave Theory and by far the most in-depth is Pretcher and Frost's, *Elliott Wave Principle*. I have attempted to give a basic education in Elliott Wave Theory and hopefully have provided enough information to make it a useful component in an overall investment strategy. I once again want to apologize for causing the impulse to count waves in all charts. I want to mention that EWT can be applied to other indicators as well and are not just used for stock prices. EWT used in conjunction with Fibonacci ratios can also provide additional insight into price projections and reversal points.

Fibonacci

Elliott used the Fibonacci sequence and ratios to build EWT which is a key component to understand. Most books will give a background history of Fibonacci, but I will forgo this and jump straight in to the details of his numbers and philosophy. First is the Fibonacci sequence which he developed while attempting to answer the question of how many rabbits can be produced over a year starting with a pair? From this study came is famous sequence of numbers. They are:

1, 1, 2, 3, 5, 8, 13, 21, 34, 55, 89, and 144 on to infinity. These numbers are a sequence in which the last number is added to the previous number to arrive at the next number.

The Golden Ratio

The sequence of numbers provides an interesting relationship. Take any number from the sequence and divide it by the preceding number and the result will be a number that is close to 1.618. For example 89/55 = 1.618. The reciprocal of 1.618 is .618 and can be obtained by taking any number in the sequence and dividing by the number that follows it, 55/89 = .618. This ratio has interesting mathematical properties such as being the only number that when added to 1 is the same as 1 divided by itself and if 0.618 is multiplied by 1.618 it is equal to 1.

The Golden ratio has been used in many applications, from the building of the great pyramids to identifying a beautiful face. It has been said that the golden ratio is the ratio that is most pleasing to the human eye. When observers see a structure or a face that is in proportion to the golden ratio, they tend to find it attractive. Great architects have used the ratio for designing buildings and painters have used it to construct great works of art. It has been shown that even the human body is constructed very close to this ratio. To support this, with a tape measure, measure a person's height from head to toe then measure from the bellybutton to the top of the head. Notice that the latter measurement is 0.618 of the total height. Almost all of nature has this Golden ratio ranging from sea shells to the shape of a hurricane. What does this ratio have to do with charts? The Golden ratio as well as other related ratios can help in determining price objectives or targets in both down and up moves.

Assume there is a bull market, and investors are counting Motive waves up. Locate a corrective wave 2 and begin wave labeling of A, B and C. Is it possible to hypothesize on what level the price will stop once wave 2 is complete? If a Zigzag pattern develops, look for a retracement of wave 1 of about 61.8%, which is .618. Look back at the discussion of Dow Theory and notice he used a ratio for retracements of about 33% to 66% for correction of the Primary Trend. Elliott determined that the correction is more directly related to Fibonacci than Dow had observed. This is remarkable to me that these great pioneers in technical analysis observed over long periods of time that markets have a pattern of retracing roughly 33% to 66% of the previous trend. In Fibonacci terms we would use 38.2% and 61.8% in place of Dow's 33% to 66%. Keep in mind that these levels of retracement are tendencies and should not be confused with hard fast rules. With experience investors will learn to use these levels to buy a particular stock or to exit a stock that has been held for profit. Do not attempt to use these levels for buy and sell signals alone as they can fluctuate and at time fail to materialize.

Break down the corrective phase into its A, B, and C components and see the additional relationships. Use these relationships to fine tune price target projections. Remember that a typical corrective wave will correct the previous trend by roughly 38.2% to 61.8%. In a Zigzag, wave C is often the same length as wave A, but when there is a variance, often wave C may fall short of the length of wave A and only move 61.8% of the wave A move, or wave C may be 1.618 or 161.8% the length of wave A. If wave C appears to have bottomed and the Primary trend is now resuming, take a few of these Fibonacci relationships to see if the move was within the parameters to confirm that the probability of a resuming Primary trend is likely. There are many more relationships for corrective waves, and if interested an analyst should seek out additional resources if this is the selected area of study.

Fibonacci ratios are often used in Motive waves as well. For example the impulse waves of a Motive wave tend to be related based in some way by 2.618, 1.618, .618, or .382. There are several examples of relationships that EWT practitioners claim to occur often. Some claim that if wave 1 and wave 5 are similar in length, wave 3 will likely be 1.618 to 2.618 the length of waves 1 and 5. There are so many relationships that have been observed in the markets that it would be unfeasible to print them all and impractical to even consider.

I have studied EWT for several years and personally believe it is too easy to misinterpret to be a practical investing tool. I am not saying that it is useless by any means. I am saying that wave counts are often realized only when they have occurred and that any trading signals would often be late when compared to other technical parameters. Even experienced EWT practitioners often argue of the current wave count and structure making interpretation even more difficult for the beginner. All is not lost for those interested in EWT. It can be used alongside other technical indicators to help time entry and exits from either the market as a whole or individual stocks. For example, assume an investor is following a stock that has entered a corrective period. He or she believes the stock is one that will improve over the long period and would be a good addition to existing holdings. An understanding of EWT and the Fibonacci ratios can create a target price the stock should fall to during this corrective period. If the stock does fall to the target price based on a retracement of the primary trend of 61.8% and the investor subsequently gets a buy signal on other technical indicators, he or she can be confident that the retracement was correct and go ahead with addition purposes.

Point and Figure

Point and Figure (PF) charting is similar to the bar chart and other charting techniques as it gives recognizable patterns, but it varies greatly because it contains no variable for time. PF charting is often used for longer term investing and is completely unique to the stock market. The characteristics of PF charts as described by Jeremy Du Plessis in his book *The Definitive Guide to Point and Figure* are as follows:

- Most of the time they are constructed with Xs and Os
- Xs are used for up moves
- Os are used for down moves
- The Xs and Os are what are referred to as boxes
- Each X and O represents a discrete price interval, which is called the box size.
- Price changes below this box size interval are ignored when plotting the chart
- A column of Xs changes to a column of Os (and vice versa) when the price changes direction by a given number of boxes. Tis is called the 'reversal size'.
- The columns of Xs and Os represent demand and supply.
- The chart sensitivity can be varied to show the short, medium and long-term position using th same data by varying the box size.
- Price gaps are recorded as if the price traded through the gap.
- Price is scaled on the vertical Y axis
- There is no time-scale along the horizontal X axis.
- Time plays no part in the construction or analysis of Point and Figure charts.
- Although there is no time axis, Pint and Figure charts are two-dimensional charts because the x-axis advances as the price reverses direction.
- Volume plays no part in the construction of Point and Figure charts

- Point and Figure charts are named according to their box and reversal size.

As outlined in the above characteristics, PF charts do not display a time scale nor do they display volume which gives them their unique nature. Figure 1.7 is an example of a PF chart.

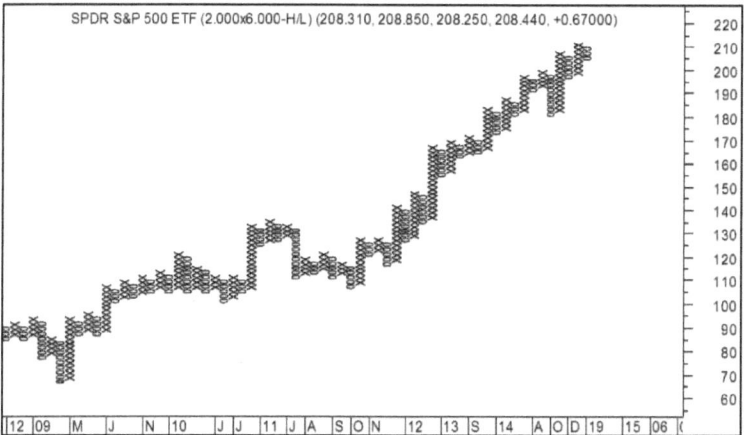

Figure 15.7

An easy way to remember why the Xs and Os are called boxes is to picture Figure 15.7 as a sheet of graph paper, and each X or O can only occupy one box on the sheet of graph paper, hence the name box.

The **Box size** represents the change in value that must take place in order for another X or O to be placed in a box. It can be thought of as the sensitivity value. For example in Figure 15.7 the box size is two, and in order for another O to be placed below the current O on the far right side of the chart, the price must fall from $208 to $206. If a box size was 25, the values for a line of ascending Xs would be 25, 50, 75, 100, and 125 and on and on. If the price goes from 25 to 45 there would not be another X since the price did not move equal to or above the box size.

The **Reversal Amount** is also a measure of sensitivity and is the number of boxes required to change from a column of Xs to a column of Os or vise versa. The most common reversal sizes are 1-box and 3-box; however, at times even 5-box PF charts are used. If there is a Box size of 25 and a reversal size of 1, to reverse from a column of Xs to a Column of Os, the price would need to fall by 25, or to reverse from a column of Os to a column of Xs the price would need to rise by 25. If the reversal size was 3 instead of 1, the price would need to fall by 75 (25*3) in order to change a column of Xs to a column of Os and would need to rise by 75 to change a column of Os to a column of Xs. So an investor needs only to multiply the box size by the reversal size to obtain the reversal amount.

The great asset of PF charts is that they are objective by nature as opposed to standard bar charts that are subjective. The 1-box PF chart is somewhat subjective as will be demonstrated later, but the 3-box is completely objective. The reason 1-box PF charts are susceptible to subjectivity is due to their sensitivity. Figures 14.8 and 14.9 show the difference between 1-box and 3-box.

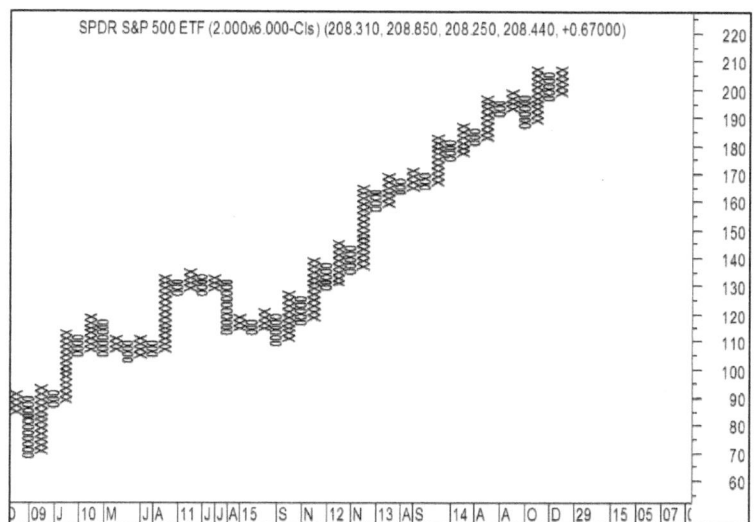

Figure 15 8 3-Box Reversal Size

Figure 15.9 1-Box Reversal Size

Notice both Figure 15.8 and Figure 15.9 show the same chart with the same price data; however, the 1-box chart is more sen-sitive to price movement than is the 3-box chart. The following text will prove why 3-box charts are totally objective by nature and the 1-box have a little subjectivity to them.

Point and Figure Signals and Patterns

The best feature of PF charts is that when a buy or sell signal is generated, it is unquestionable. The downside is that because the signal is unquestionable does not mean it will result in a trip to the bank. PF charts make interpretation easy and less time consuming than traditional bar charts. Observe the main signals generated from PF charts.

Double-Top and Double-Bottom Signals

Double-Top and Bottom buy and sell signals are the easiest to identify, but do not confuse the terminology of the PF Double-Top and Bottom with that of regular bar charts since double top and bottom patterns in bar charts represent reversal signals. Figure 15.10 highlights the Double-Top and Double Bottom Signals in a 1-box reversal PF chart.

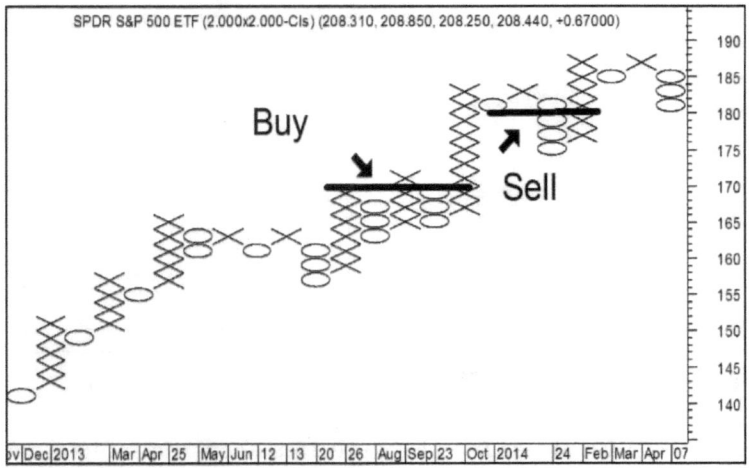

Figure 15.10

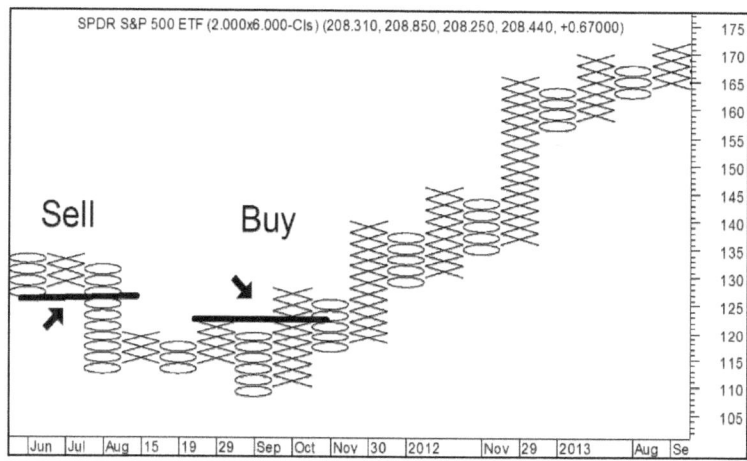

Figure 15.11

Figure 15.11 represent the 3-box reversal Double-Top buy and Double-Bottom sell signals.

Triple-Top and Triple-Bottom Patterns

The Triple-Top and Triple-Bottom patterns are identical to the Double-top and Double-Bottom patterns with the exceptions the Triple-Top and Bottom patterns hold more weight and increase the probability of success than the Double-Top and Bottom patterns. The reason for this is the stronger support and resistance before the breakout. Figure 15.12 is a typical Triple-Top and Bottom signals in a 3-box PF chart.

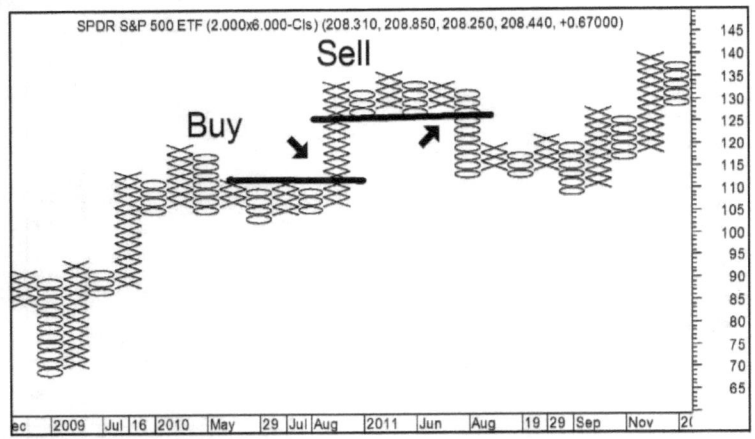

Figure 15.12

Study the chart above for a moment and remember what I said about the Triple-Top and Bottom patterns; they carry more weight. As demonstrated in Figure 15.12, the Triple-Bottom sell did not hold up, and the Triple-top buy created a whipsaw trade. I believe it is important to show reality rather than perfect charts which only show perfect signals that work. In reality signals and indicators fail, and I feel it is my job to not only help investors learn the basics of investing, whether it is fundamental or technical and to show real life signals whether they workout as planned or whether they fail. Notice that several charts that I show indicate that a particular signal was generated, but the trade signal failed and the price moved in the opposite direction. When looking at these charts, do not think there is a lack of understanding the signal, but instead be proud of noticing a failure without having it pointed out.

Other Patterns

There are numerous patterns for both the 1-box and 3-box PF charts, and since this is an introduction to technical analysis and the 1-box PF charts require experience, I will focus the remainder of this chapter on the 3-box PF charts. The same patterns studied in previous chapters can be seen in PF charts. The classic Head and Shoulders pattern can be identified in PF charts, as can be seen in Figure 15.13

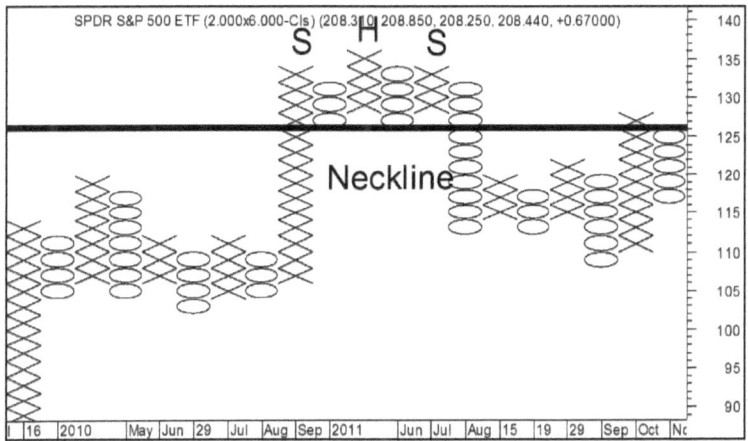

Figure 15.13

Trend lines can be drawn and are used in a similar method as for bar charts. Triangles can be seen in PF charts and are often in the form of a Symmetrical Triangle studied in previous chapters. The signal is generated when the PF chart breaks out of the Triangle in either direction and one of the classic PF signals occurs such as a Double-Top or Bottom buy or sell signal. Catapults occur when a PF chart signals a buy signal from say a Triple-Top then falls back below the buy signal but does not trigger a sell signal. It will then generate a Double-Top buy signal. This is a Catapult.

One of the most interesting features of PF is the ease with which investors can create price targets. There are two methods of doing this, the Horizontal Count and the Vertical Count. I will start with the Horizontal Count. Notice what are called Walls and are pictured in Figure 15.14.

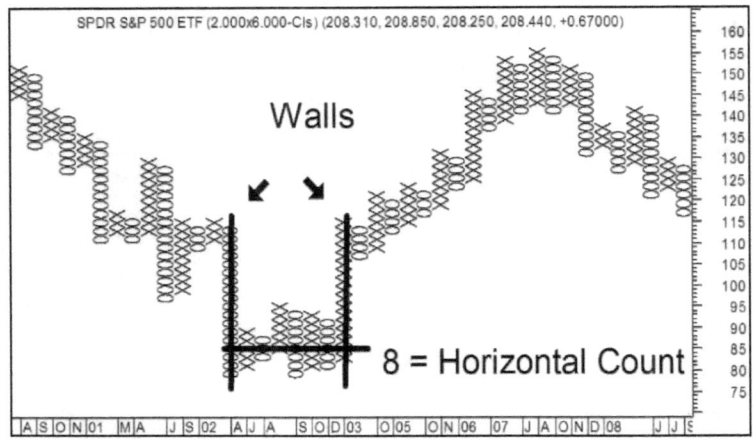

Figure 15.14

Add the number of columns that are between these two walls. In this example there are eight. We multiply the horizontal count by the reversal amount (3) and multiply this sum by the box size, which is two in this case. Take this number and add it to the lowest point in the column that breaks out. In Figure 14.14 the price target would be:

$$8 * 3 * 2 = 48 + 83 = 131$$

The price target from Figure 15.14 is thus $131.00 which it attains and continues to move higher once the price target is reached. The price target is not a sell signal; it is used to determine if the buy signal is worth investors' time and money. If the price target would net a profit of five dollars but the transaction cost would be seven dollars, an investor would likely forego the investment and look for more profitable trades. The Horizontal count can be used with both 1-box and 3-box PF charts.

Vertical Count

The Vertical Count can only be used with the 3-box PF chart. The Vertical Count is calculated by taking the number of boxes in the column that generated a buy or sell signal, multiply it by three (the reversal amount), and multiply this by the box size. Figure 15.15 shows an example of a vertical count. The formula is:

$$17 * 3 * 2 = 102 + 83 = 185$$

The Vertical Count price target is $185, which is more than $50 higher than what was obtained from the Horizontal Count. An investor could use the more conservative count of $131 until this price target was reached and switch to the more aggressive price target. I will say that the $185 price target was never reached, so investors cannot hold to a price target once a sell signal or reversal pattern has been displayed. Recall from the chapter on behavioral finance to avoid anchoring to a number, especially a price target.

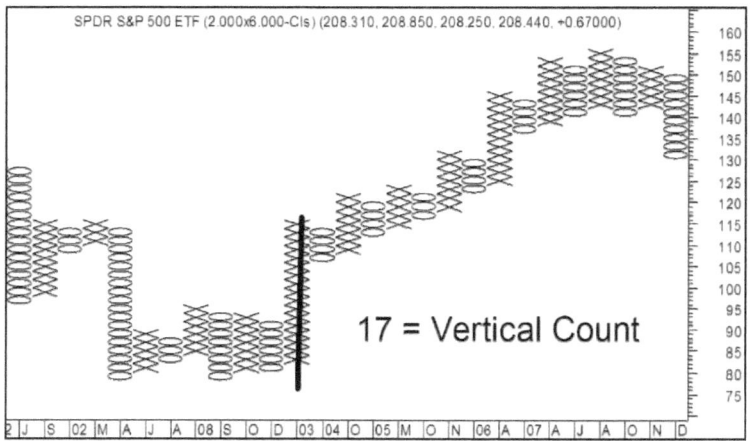

Figure 15.15

Point and Figure charts are unique because they do not display volume or time and thus focus only on price. The 3-box PF charts are objective whereas the 1-box PF charts contain an element of subjectivity. The classic patterns studied in an earlier chapter can be used in PF charts and must be confirmed with a PF buy or sell signal in order to be acted upon. PF charts can be extremely useful to the analyst who takes the time to study the methodology. Jeremy Du Plessis has written a fantastic book that investigates the subject matter called, *The Definitive Guide to Point and Figure.*

[16]

Conclusion

I wrote this book not to give my opinion although I am afraid it came through more than I would have liked. My objective is to give the reader a multifaceted look at the investment world. If reading this as a Financial Advisor, I hope to have sparked some interest that he or she will share with clients to help them achieve their long term financial goals. If an individual bought this book hoping to find a definitive answer to the best way to "beat the market" or settle the debate between active and passive management or MPT and Behavioral Finance, he or she was likely disappointed. I wanted to show advisors as well as individual investors that there actually is no right or wrong way to invest when considering whether to be an active or passive investor; it comes down to what the investor believes is possible and what any investor believes he or she or an advisor is capable of achieving. As an advisor to individual clients and a consultant to other financial advisors, I tend to lean on a combination of both active and passive. I have seen both methods go through turmoil only to be redeemed when most investors have given up hope. In the aftermath of 2008, most media outlets as well as advisors that I consulted believe Modern Portfolio Theory had run its course as it had appeared to have broken down during the crisis. Nearly every client and advisor I met with wanted only to talk about my tactical approach to investing; they did not want to hear the words "buy and hold" ever again. What has happened since then? Since the bottom of the market crash in March of 2009, the market has gained back all of its losses and some. What strategy performed the best during this time period? MPT or Passive. Most active strategies who have been tactical or used technical analysis have underperformed the broad markets. This is mostly due to very small corrections that caused technical analyst to sell only to be lured back into the market at a higher price, which is called a whipsaw. The same clients and advisors who did not want to hear the words "buy and hold" are now starting to think they have made the wrong decision and that active management has once again been a lost cause.

As humans we tend to swing like a pendulum from one ex-treme to the other. When investors believe they need to make a switch from active to passive, the markets will once again prove them wrong. I believe the most important element of a sound investment strategy is one where emotional biases can be minimized. Advisors need to educate clients about these pitfalls because of the dramatic impact they have on investor portfolios. If investors are managing their own assets, they must remember to journal and keep a list of these emotional biases nearby and refer to them often. It is advisable to de-velop a strategy and thereby eliminate as many biases as pos-sible.

Some may have read this book and decided it is too much work to properly manage a portfolio and that it would be well worth paying a professional to implement an investment strategy. This is an excellent conclusion, and I often recommend seeking professional help especially if an investor prefers to spend free time on the golf course as opposed to studying company finan-cial statements or monitoring stock charts. This book should serve as a valuable reference when interviewing investment managers. For example, if an advisor claims to be an active manager and charges a fee for this service, ask them questions from this book. Ask how they plan to obtain a residual return, or what is their methodology for picking individual stocks? If the subject is avoided or not answered directly and to complete satisfaction, move on, do not stay with an advisor because there is a personal or professional relationship. Pick an advisor as one would pick a surgeon. This book and its advice will be more appreciated at that point.

It will not be hard to find a financial advisor that manages portfolios passively. One thing to remember is that buying and holding mutual funds that are supposed to be actively managed does not constitute active portfolio management. I believe that passive strategy should use indexed ETFs or indexed mutual funds that are low cost, not active mutual funds that are expensive and often, over time become so large that they maintain a higher fee but begin to track the index much closer.

My goal is that an investor can take what he has learned from this book and build a portfolio or work with an investment advisor to implement an investment strategy. If the reader is an investment advisor, I hope he or she is able to add strategies to a personal advisory practice and is able to help both active and passive investors while taking what has been learned from this book and developing strategies that make clients happy. I did not write this book thinking that a person near retirement would be able to read this book and implement an investment strategy with zero experience. I wrote this book geared toward advisors who may not have been in the portfolio management business but would like to branch out from selling strategies to building strategies. It is also suitable for the do-it-yourselfer investor who has experience with markets but wants to move past buying individual stocks with no direction to an informed strategy of when to buy, what to buy, and of course, when to sell.

I believe that after reading this book investors or managers should have a basic knowledge of the pieces necessary to build a successful investment strategy. By combining valuation concepts with technical analysis and tying it all together with portfolio management, I see no reason an investor cannot design and implement a sound investment strategy. I hope this book is the foundation and beginning of a quest for investment knowledge and the beginning of a very profitable investing future.

References

Blum, L., and S. Drulauf. 2007. *The New Palgrave: A Dictionary of Economics.* New York: Palgrave McMillan.

Blume, Marshall. 1971. "On the Assessment of Risk." *The Journal of Finance* 26 (1): 1-10.

Bodie, Zvi, Alex Kane, and Alan Marcus. 2013. *Investments.* Maidenhead: McGraw-Hill Education.

Campbell, John Y. , and Robert Shiller. 1988. "Stock Prices, Earnings and Expected Dividends." *Journal of Finance* 43: 661-76.

Dechow, Patricia, AMy Hutton, and Richard Sloan. 1999. "An Empirical Assessment of the Residual Income Valuation Model." *Journal of Accounting and Economics* 26: 1-34.

DeFusco, R, W Mcleavey, J Pinto, and D Runkle. 2007. *Quantitative Investment Analysis.* 2nd. Hoboken: John Wiley & Sons, Inc.

Edwards, Robert, and John Magee. 1948. *Technical Analysis of Stock Trends.* BN Publishing.

Fama, E, and K French. 1993. "Common Risk Factors in the Returns on Stocks and Bonds." *Journal of Financial Economics* 33 (1): 3-56.

Fama, E, and K French. 2004. "The Capital Asset Pricing Model: Theory and Evidence." *Journal of Economic Perspectives* 18 (3): 25-46.

Fama, Eugene F, and Kenneth R French. 1989. "Business Conditions and Expected Returns on Stocks and Bonds." *Journal of Financial Economics* 25: 3-22.

Fuller, Russell, and Chi-Cheng Hsia. 1984. "A Simplified Common Stock Valuation Model." *Financial Analyst Journal* 40 (5): 49-56.

Gordon, Myron. 1959. "Dividends, Earnings and Stock Prices." *Review of Economics and Statistics* 41 (2): 99-105.

Hall, Crystal C, Lynn Ariss, and Alexander Todorov. 2005. *The illusion of knowledge: When more information reduces accuracy and increases confidence.* Psychology, Princeton: ScienceDirect.

Howard, C. Thomas. 2014. *Behavioral Portfolio Management.* Petersfield: Harriman House LTD.

Ibbotson, Roger, and Peng Chen. 2003. "Long-Run Stock Returns: Participating in the Real Economy." *Financial Analyst Journal* 58 (1): 88-98.

Kahn, R., and R Grinold. 1999. *Active Portfolio Management: A Quantitative Approach for Producing Superior Returns and Controling Risk.* New York: McGraw-Hill.

Kahneman, Daniel. 2011. *Thinking Fast and Slow.* New York: Farrar, Straus and Giroux.

Kirkpatrick II, Charles D, and Julie Jahlquist. 2011. *Technical Analysis.* Upper Saddle River: Pearson Education, Inc.

Lo, Andrew. 2004. "The Adaptive Market Hypothesis: Market Efficiency from an Evolutionary Perspective." *The Journal of Portfolio Management* 30 (5): 15-29.

Lohse, Davis F, and J. Kottemann. 1994. "Harmful Effects of seemingly helpful information on forecasts of stock earnings." *Journal of Economic Psychology* 15 (2): 253-267.

Markowitz, Harry. 1952. "Portolio Selection." *Journal of Finance* 7 (1): 77-91.

—. 2014. *Risk-Return Analysis.* New York: McGraw-Hill.

Montier, James. 2007. *Behavioural Investing: A Practitioners Guide to Applying Behavioural Finance.* West Sussex: John Wiley & Sons Ltd.

Morris, Gregory. 2006. *The complete Guide to Market Breadth Indicators.* New York: McGraw-Hill.

O'Creevy, M, N Nicholson, E Soane, and P Willman. 2003. "Trading on Illusions: Unrealistic Perceptions of Control and Trading Performance." *Journal of Occupational and Organizational Psychology* 76 (1): 53-68.

Pinto, J, E Henry, T Robinson, and J Stowe. 2010. *Equity Asset Valuation.* New Jersey: Nohn Wiley & Sons, Inc.

Plessis, Jeremy Du. 2005. *The Definitive Guide to Point and Figure.* Petersfield: Harriman House.

Porter, M. E. 1979. *How competitive Forces Shape Strategy.* Harvard Business Review.

Prechter, Robert, and A. J. Frost. 2005. *Elliot Wave Principle.* Gainesville: New Classics Library.

Pring, Martin. 2014. *Technical Analysis Explained.* New York: McGraw-Hill Education.

Simonsohn, U., N Karlsson, G Loewenstein, and D Ariely. 2008. "The Tree of Experience in the Forest of Information: Overweighing experienced relative to observed information." *Games & Economic Behavior* 62 (1): 263-286.

Skinner, B. F. 1947. "Superstition in the Pigeon." *Journal of Experimental Psychology* 38: 168-172.

Treynor, Jack L, and F Black. 1973. "How to Use Security Analysis to Improve Portfolio Selection." *Journal of Business* 66-88.

Williams, J. 1938. *The Theory of Investment Value.* BN Publishing.

Index

NOTES

NOTES

NOTES

NOTES

www.ingramcontent.com/pod-product-compliance
Lightning Source LLC
Chambersburg PA
CBHW021403170526
45164CB00002B/481